Decorative Sewing

Decorative Sewing

Embellish Almost Anything with Appliqué, Beading, Cross-Stitch, and More

Sarah Beaman

The Reader's Digest Association, Inc.
Pleasantville, New York/Montreal

For my mum, Ann—with love and thanks for teaching me how to sew.

A READER'S DIGEST BOOK

This edition published by The Reader's Digest Association, Inc., by arrangement with Anova Books

FOR ANOVA BOOKS
Commissioning Editor: Michelle Lo
Designer Manager: Gemma Wilson
Editor: Kate Haxell
Designer: Andrew Easton for Talking Design
Photography: Matthew Dickens
Illustrations: Kang Chen

FOR READER'S DIGEST
U.S. Project Editor: Kimberly Casey
Copy Editor: Mary Connell
Consulting Editor: Jane Townswick
Project Designer: Jennifer Tokarski
Cover Designer: Mabel Zorzano
Canadian Project Editor: Pamela Johnson
Associate Art Director: George McKeon
Executive Editor, Trade Publishing: Dolores York
President and Publisher: Harold Clarke

Library of Congress Cataloging in Publication Data:

Beaman, Sarah.
    Decorative Sewing : embellish almost anything with appliqué, beading, cross-stitch, and more / Sarah Beaman.
    p. cm.
    ISBN-13: 978-0-7621-0667-7
    ISBN-10: 0-7621-0667-0
    1. Fancy work. 2. Textile crafts. I. Title.
TT570.B4155 2006
746.4—dc22
                                                                    2006049346

Address any comments about *Decorative Sewing* to:
The Reader's Digest Association, Inc.
Adult Trade Publishing
Reader's Digest Road
Pleasantville, NY 10570-7000

For more Reader's Digest products and information, visit our website:
www.rd.com (in the United States)
www.readersdigest.ca (in Canada)

Reproduction by Anorax
Printed and bound by WKT Co. Ltd, China

1 3 5 7 9 10 8 6 4 2

NOTE TO OUR READERS
The editors who produced this book have attempted to make the contents as accurate and correct as possible.
Illustrations, photographs, and text have been carefully checked. All instructions should be reviewed and understood
by the reader before undertaking any project. The directions and designs for the projects in this publication are under copyright.
These projects may be reproduced for the reader's personal use or for gifts. Reproduction for sale or profit is forbidden by law.

Contents

Introduction

Decorative sewing can be a delightfully rewarding experience. Whether you are just a beginner who is still learning basic embroidery stitches or have mastered more advanced sewing, patchwork, and beading techniques over the years, you'll delight in the wonderful sense of achievement to be derived from creating glamorous and fashionable clothing items from scratch or adding novel embellishments to purchased garments and home furnishings.

The sections of this book are dedicated to a range of decorative possibilities. Start by reading through the section on equipment, and gather together the tools and supplies you'll use in learning the techniques that follow. Then, move on to the technique chapters, and use the step-by-step photos to guide you as you experiment with each technique and add new sewing skills to your repertoire of favorites. Then, try making the projects that feature those techniques. Each project is fully explained in clear step-by-step instructions and fully illustrated to guide you easily through every stage of production. Finally, enjoy browsing through the ideas gallery for each technique and let the colorful photos inspire you to create beautifully decorated sewing projects.

If you are a beginner, have fun experimenting! Try combining different fabrics and embellishing them with various sewing techniques to create simple projects of your own imagination. Then enjoy receiving compliments for their charm.

If you are a more experienced sewer, the expert techniques and ideas you'll find here will become a springboard for your own further creative leaps of imagination.

Happy sewing!

Sarah

Equipment

If you are an avid sewer, you probably already have a wide range of specialized sewing tools at hand. If you are a beginner, you will only need a minimum of basic equipment and tools to get you started; there is no need to rush out and spend a fortune on top-quality tools. As you tackle projects over time, you will slowly acquire quite a collection, and many of them will become old and reliable favorites to meet your sewing needs.

It's your choice whether you would rather sew by hand or use a sewing machine to create projects. You can, of course, embellish commercial clothing or home furnishings using hand-stitching techniques, but a sewing machine with built-in creative features will vastly extend your possibilities. You'll also be able to construct your own unique projects from scratch. If you do plan to buy a machine, choose a model that can produce zigzag, buttonhole, and other creative stitches as well as ordinary straight stitches.

General-purpose sewing equipment

Dressmaker's scissors Designed with bent handles and long blades, these scissors allow fabric to be cut quickly using the smallest number of cuts. Never use them to cut paper, because they will blunt very quickly.

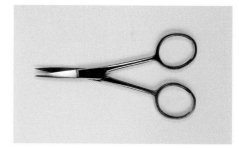

Embroidery scissors These scissors have short, sharp blades for trimming threads. They are also useful for cutting small areas of fabric or intricate details; they're ideal for cutting buttonholes.

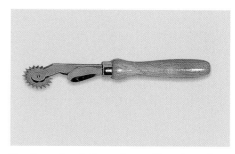

Tracing wheel Great for making slotted perforations. It is used with or without tracing paper and can transfer markings from paper to paper, or paper to fabric.

Pinking shears Designed with notched blades, these shears cut a zigzag edge that will help prevent fraying, and offer a quick way of finishing raw edges of fabrics.

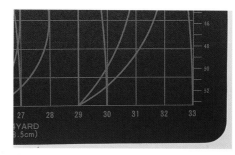

Cutting mat Designed for both rotary blades and straight utility blades; a mat provides a long-lasting, nonglare surface that can be cut and slashed constantly without showing marks.

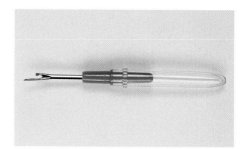

Seam ripper Use the ripper's sharp-pointed prong to push through stitches and cut with the tiny, curved blade. It's an ideal tool for removing basting stitches and ripping out incorrectly sewn stitches.

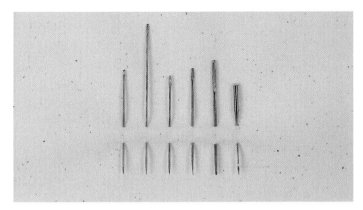

Left to right:

- **Ordinary sewing needle** Use this sharp-type needle that comes in several sizes for general purpose sewing.

- **Long darner** This ultra-long needle type is good for basting and hand-gathering. You can pick up a lot of stitches at a time.

- **Small-eyed embroidery needle** This is good for embroidering with floss and other fine embroidery threads.

- **Large-eyed embroidery needle** Use this with chunkier embroidery yarn, such as soft embroidery cotton and Persian wool.

- **Tapestry needle** A blunt needle with a large eye, this is useful for stitching on open-weave fabrics or threading ribbons through casings.

- **Sewing machine needle** This type of needle comes in a variety of sizes: the higher the number, the thicker the needle. Use sharp-tipped ones on woven fabrics, ball-point ones on knits, and specially designed ones for sewing leather.

Left to right:

- **Topstitching thread** A thick thread used for topstitching because it shows up well on fabric.

- **Synthetic thread** Various synthetic threads are designed to reflect the strength and elasticity of synthetic fabrics. As a general rule, try to match the fiber content of the thread to that of the fabric you are sewing.

- **Natural thread** Natural fabrics such as cotton, linen, or silk are best sewn with similar natural threads.

- **Basting thread** This fine, cotton thread breaks easily but does not tangle or knot. You can often get away with using inexpensive brands of thread for basting, but always use good quality thread for permanent stitching.

sewSMART

Glass-headed pins are more expensive than plastic ones, but they may save you money in the long run. When pressing fabric during the construction process, the heat of your iron may melt the plastic and damage the fabric.

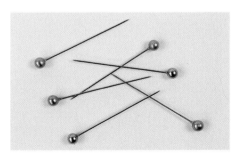

Dressmaker's glass-headed pins The large heads of these general-purpose pins make them easy to use in a project.

Extra-fine silk pins Use these pins on delicate fabrics to avoid making damaging holes in them.

Marking tools

Left to right:

- **Roll-along chalk dispenser** Chalk wheels make a fine powder line on fabrics that can easily be brushed away. Chalk is available in different colors and the dispenser can be refilled when empty.

- **Chalk pencil** Marks left by this pencil can be brushed away when the stitching is finished.

- **Water-erasable marking pen** Marks made by this pen can be removed by lightly sponging or washing the fabric, so it may not be suitable for dry-clean-only fabrics.

- **Air-erasing marking pen** This pen makes marks that fade away. Depending on the fabric being used, this can happen slowly or quickly. Test on your fabrics to determine whether the marks will remain visible for the duration of the stitching process.

- **Silver marking pencil** The silver color shows up on many fabrics and the marks made by this pencil can be washed out.

- **Carbon transfer pencil** This pencil is suitable for transfering a motif onto fabric (see page 39).

sewSMART

There are many types of fabric markers available. Before using a marker in a project, always test it first on a scrap of the same fabric or in an inconspicuous location.

General Sewing Tips

- Choose the right fabric for your project—one with characteristics that will suit the purpose of the item. If you are unsure, seek advice when you purchase your materials.

- Measure twice, cut once.

- Before you start any project, think ahead and plan your construction sequence carefully.

- Be sure you have enough fabrics before you start.

- Always check the settings of your sewing machine before you begin to sew. Test the tension and stitch length on a scrap of fabric for your project.

- If you are not going to baste sections together, use plenty of pins to hold them securely and remove them just before you stitch over them.

- Stitch accurately, always taking the correct seam allowance.

Beading equipment

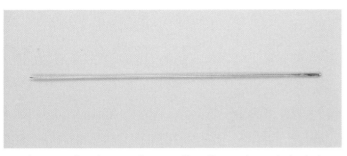

Beading needle This very fine needle will pass through the holes of the tiniest beads.

Beading thread Fine and strong, this thread is flat, so it can pass through the eye of a beading needle. It is made especially for beading, but comes in a limited color range.

Bead scoop Picking up tiny beads can be difficult. You can buy special scoops for this purpose, but a teaspoon works just as well.

Beading mat This mat has a pile surface that stops beads from rolling around; a square of velvet glued to thick cardboard makes an acceptable alternative.

Patchwork and quilting equipment

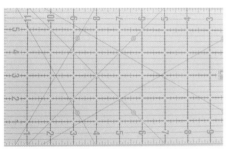

Quilter's ruler This acrylic ruler is marked in a grid of squares and has lines at various angles, making it a versatile tool for cutting pieces of patchwork fabric.

Embroidery hoop Available in various sizes and shapes, this type is a must for hand embroidery and is very useful for beaded embroidery, too.

Rotary cutter The rolling blade of this cutter makes a smooth, continuous cut. Work on a self-healing cutting mat to protect your work surface.

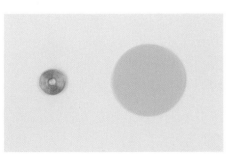

- **Quilter's disk** Use this with a template to mark the seam allowance. Place the disk edge against the template edge, put a pencil in the hole, and wheel it around the edge of the template.
- **Needle grabber** This thin rubber patch will help you grip a needle and pull it through the thickest fabric.

Embroidery

Worked by hand or machine, embroidery is a fantastic way to embellish any item, and this exciting craft is gaining in popularity today. You don't need to be an expert to combine fabrics artfully with embroidery threads in a myriad of colors. Whether you start a project from scratch or simply apply a unique decorative touch to a purchased item, you're sure to enjoy the results of your handiwork and creativity.

Hand embroidery

Hand embroidery—working decorative stitches on a fabric surface—is one of the most popular ways of adding interesting details to garments and home fashions. Many hand embroidery stitches require only basic sewing skills, and they are simple enough for a beginner to tackle. Start out using simple backstitches or cross-stitches and as your confidence and skills develop, move on to more difficult stitches.

Preparing Fabric

With care, hand or machine embroidery stitches can be worked on almost any type of fabric, from delicate tulle to heavyweight wool. If the project is to be laundered regularly, pretreat your fabric to ensure that all of it will be washable and colorfast. If the fabric is very lightweight, you can provide extra stability for the stitches by working through two layers of fabric. These don't have to be the same, but they do need to be compatible. When working with transparent or semitransparent fabrics, consider how the stitches will look from the right side, and be careful when carrying threads across the back of your design (called "traveling") and finishing the ends. In the case of both hand and machine stitching, be sure that the tension is not too tight, or it will distort the surface of the fabric. Using an embroidery hoop can help to prevent this.

Binding an embroidery hoop

Binding an embroidery hoop with a strip of muslin or plain cotton fabric will create an even tension across the surface of the fabric being worked and prevent it from slipping in the process.

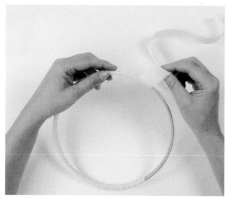

1 Tear a 1 in. (2.5 cm)-wide strip of un-dyed cotton or muslin fabric. Hold one end of the strip against the inside of the inner ring and wrap the strip over the end to secure it in place. Wrap the strip smoothly and evenly around the inner ring.

2 Continue binding around the ring. When you reach the starting point, cut off any excess fabric. Wrap a piece of masking or cloth adhesive tape tightly and smoothly over the cut end of the fabric to hold it in place.

3 The bound inner ring fits snugly inside the outer ring of the embroidery hoop. The screw fitting can easily be adjusted to accommodate fabrics of very different thicknesses.

Hand embroidery threads and yarns

For the best results, take the characteristics of the background fabric into account and choose embroidery threads to complement. Visualize the finished result— a matte linen thread may work well on a linen background, but looks less appropriate on a silky synthetic cloth.

Left to right:

- **Tapestry wool** A non-divisible 4-ply wool yarn with a soft "hand" ideal for creative stitching.
- **Persian wool** A divisible 3-ply yarn that produces a soft effect.
- **Silk embroidery ribbon** A specialty item, flat silk ribbon is available in several widths and is ideal for raised effects.
- **Soft embroidery cotton** Thick thread used for a full, matte finish.
- **Variegated embroidery cotton** A medium-weight thread dyed in different shades, so stitches will change color as you sew.
- **Cotton perlé** A nondivisible, lustrous yarn with a high twist and smooth finish.
- **Variegated cotton perlé** A multicolored version.
- **Coton à broder** A lightweight, smooth thread in many shades.
- **Variegated coton à broder** Multicolored and shaded versions are available.
- **Cotton stranded embroidery floss** A smooth thread with a medium sheen, it is probably the most common and widely available.
- **Variegated cotton stranded embroidery floss** Variegated threads that produce stitches that change color as they are worked. Multicolored and shaded types are available.
- **Hand-dyed variegated cotton stranded embroidery floss** Available from specialty suppliers, these are often dyed using vegetable dyes to produce beautiful, subtle hues.
- **Linen stranded embroidery floss** A flat, matte thread similar in construction to the cotton variety.
- **Rayon stranded embroidery floss** This springy thread has a high-sheen finish and produces a rich look. It is a stranded thread that can be separated for finer work.
- **Polyester, metallic-effect stranded embroidery floss** Synthetic thread produced in a variety of novelty finishes. The above example has a metallic finish.
- **Metal stranded embroidery floss** This contains real metal, which is wrapped around a synthetic filament for strength and recovery. It has the unmistakable appearance of real metal.
- **Lurex and rayon embroidery floss** This shiny thread is a mixture of high-shine lurex and glossy rayon filaments, and has a drapey quality. Due to its chainstitch construction, the strands cannot be separated.
- **Fine metallic braid** This is a blend of different-colored synthetic filaments. Its springy quality can make it difficult to handle.

Starting and stopping a line of stitches

Avoid beginning and ending stitching with a knot; the lump is often be visible from the front, particularly after pressing.

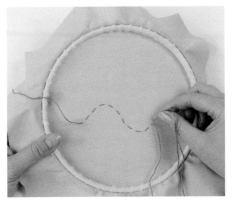

1 Bring the needle through the fabric from back to front at the point where you want to start stitching. Leave a 4 in. (10 cm) tail of thread at the back of the work. Work a short line of stitching.

2 Thread another needle with the tail of thread on the back of the work. Weave the tail through the backs of several of the stitches, then turn and weave it through the same stitches in the opposite direction. Trim the thread end. Complete the stitching on the right side and secure the end of thread in same way.

Library of Embroidery Stitches

Chain Stitch

 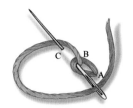

1 Come up at A. Go down to left of A, coming up at B. Loop thread under needle point from right to left.

2 Pull thread through. Go down to left of B through loop, come up at C. Loop thread as in Step 1, continue.

Detached Chain Stitch

Work a detached stitch by repeating Step 1. Pull through and make a small stitch to anchor each loop. Work five detached stitches in a circle to create a lazy daisy.

Blanket Stitch

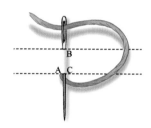 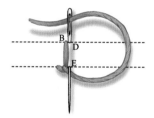 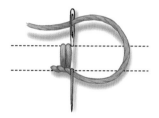

1 Come up at A, go down at B, come up at C, just to immediate right of A. Carry thread under needle point from left to right. Pull thread through.

2 Go down at D (just to immediate right of B). Come up at E, keeping thread under needle point.

3 Continue in this way along row, keeping all stitches even and close together, as shown.

Knotted Blanket Stitch

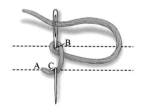 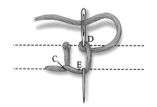

1 Come up at A. With needle over working thread form loop, go down at B, and come up directly below at C. Pull thread to form knot at top.

2 Go down through knot at D and come up at E over working thread. Pull to form another knot and continue.

Straight Stitch

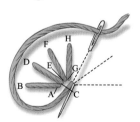

To create a straight-stitch fan, come up at A, go down at B, up at C. Repeat, going down at D, up at E, down at F, up at G, and down at H, and continue.

Running Stitch

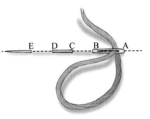

1 To create a running stitch, come up at A, go down at B, come up at C, go down at D, come up at E. Pull thread gently, so fabric does not pucker.

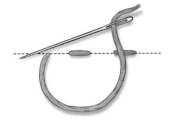

2 Continue following the design line as shown, by repeating Step 1. Keep stitches even.

Backstitch

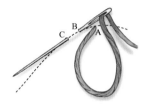

1 Working from right to left, come up at A, go down at B, then come up at C. Pull thread through.

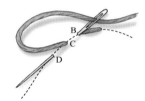

2 Go down again at B to make a backstitch, then come up at D, ready for the next stitch, and continue.

Threaded Backstitch

1 Work a row of backstitch (see left), making stitches slightly longer than normal. Use contrasting thread to weave in and out.

2 For double threaded backstitch, weave as before in opposite direction. Be careful not to split threads already worked.

Single Cross-Stitch

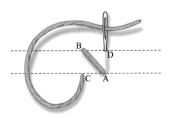

1 Come up at A, down at B, up at C, down at D. The stitch can be reversed so that the top half slants from lower right to upper left.

Working Cross-Stitch in a Row

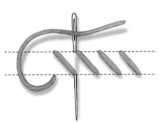

1 To work a row, make even, equally spaced diagonal stitches, working from bottom to top. Then go down at top left of previous stitch by working back across row.

2 Continue in the same manner, slanting stitches in opposite direction to form a line of crosses.

French Knot

1 Come up at A and wrap thread around needle once in counterclockwise direction.

2 Wrap thread around needle a second time in the same direction, keeping needle away from fabric.

3 Push wraps together and slide to end of needle. Insert needle close to A and pull thread through to form a French knot.

Open Fishbone Stitch

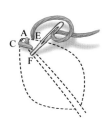

1 Come up at A and down at B, come up at C (opposite and below A), and then down at D. Follow central guidelines.

2 Come up at E, close to A. Remember to place all stitches exactly on motif outline for even edges.

3 Go down at F so that stitch lies parallel to A-B, but allow some background fabric to show through.

4 Work alternate sides to build shape. Stitches should cross each other to give consistent ridge, or leaf vein.

Raised Satin Stitch

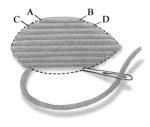

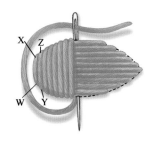

1 Come up at A, go down at B, up at C, and down at D. Continue to fill motif with basic satin stitch. Secure thread.

2 Come up at W, go down at X, up at Y, and down at Z. Continue until base stitches are completely covered.

Coral Stitch

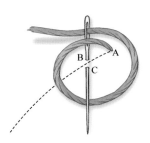

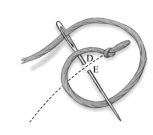

1 Come up at A and loop thread over needle, as shown. Go down at B (under thread) and up at C (over thread). Pull thread through to form knot.

2 Repeat Step 1, going down at D (under thread and up at E (over thread) as shown. Then pull thread through to form a second knot. Continue.

Feathered Chain Stitch

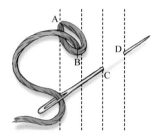

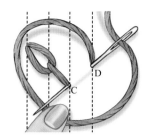

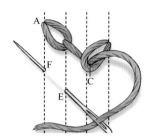

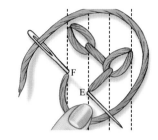

1 Come up at A. Make a loop and go down next to A, coming up through loop at B. Slant to the right, go down at C, and come up at D.

2 Pull thread through. Go down next to D, then come up at C. Loop thread under point of needle and pull thread through gently.

3 Go down at E and then come up at F (below A), as shown, to make a straight stitch. Pull thread through.

4 Go down next to F and come up at E, keeping thread under point of needle. Pull thread through.

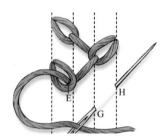

Basic Couching

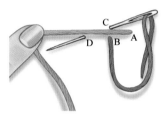

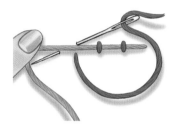

5 Go down at G and come up at H. Repeat from Step 2 to continue following the guidelines.

1 To couch a medium thread, bring it through fabric at A. (To couch a thick thread, simply lay it on fabric over design line.)

2 Using fine couching thread, come up at B; go down at C, covering laid thread; and come up at D.

3 Repeat along row, forming small stitches at right angles to laid thread.

Double Feather Stitch

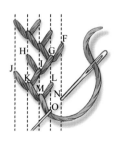

1 Come up at A, down at B, up at C, keeping needle over stitch just sewn. Repeat, following letter sequence. Then cross to left; go down at H and up at I.

2 Repeat, going down at J, up at K, down at L, up at M, down at N, up at O. Continue, working two stitches to the left and two to the right, keeping loops even.

Embroidered shirt

Simple embroidery can give a contemporary look to classic designs. In this project, basic stitches worked in subtle, muted shades, transform a plain shirt into something special. Translucent sequins add understated glamour.

Materials

- Thin paper to make a pattern
- Tracing wheel
- Compass
- Pricking mat (a mouse pad or a wad of paper towels will also work)
- Straight pin
- Air-erasing marking pen
- Stranded cotton embroidery floss in three colors to complement shirt color
- Embroidery needle
- Translucent, pearl-like sequins

Techniques

- Embroidery threads and yarns, page 15
- Backstitch, page 17
- French knot, page 18

sewSMART

An air-erasing marker is the best type to use for this project, but if you work slowly, or set the work aside for a while, the lines may disappear. If this happens, just pin the pattern in place again and draw over the lines not yet embroidered.

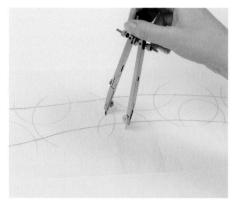

1 Lay the shirt collar flat on the paper and pin them together. Draw around the edges of the collar. Use the tracing wheel to outline the collar, and then draw marks in pencil once paper is removed.

2 Using the compass, draw a pattern of intersecting part-circles onto the paper pattern. The pattern can be symmetrical or random.

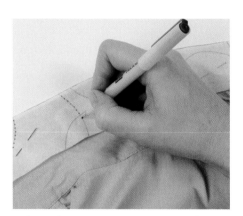

4 Pin the pattern to the collar. Mark through the pin pricks with the tip of the air-erasing marker pen to transfer the design onto the fabric. Remove the paper pattern. Embroider over the marked lines on the collar using three strands of floss and varying the colors as described. Work backstitches on some lines.

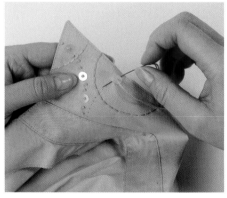

5 At random intervals attach sequins to the stitching by threading one onto the needle and making a backstitch over one side of it. Bring the needle up at the far edge of the sequin and take it down through the hole in the middle to make the next backstitch.

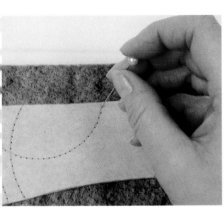

3 Cut the pattern out around the collar lines. Lay the pattern on the pricking mat and, using a straight pin, prick evenly along the drawn circles.

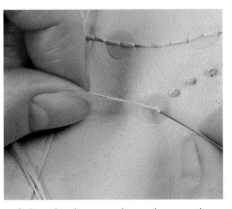

6 On other lines, work evenly spaced French knots. Again, position sequins randomly by bringing the needle up through the hole in the middle, wrapping the floss around the needle, and going back down through the hole. Work the cuffs in the same way.

Seashore wall hanging

This is an interesting way to make the most of shells and small stones collected during a walk on the beach, preserving special vacation memories. This wall hanging highlights the shapes and textures of the shells—a clever alternative to simply placing them in a dish or jar.

Materials

- 9 in. (23 cm) square of cream linen
- 9 in. (23 cm) square of sand-colored linen
- 9 x 5½ in. (23 x 14 cm) rectangle of cream linen
- Apricot, vanilla and stone-colored linen stranded-embroidery floss
- Photograph printed onto computer-compatible canvas and cut to 5½ x 9 in. (14 x 23 cm) rectangle (width by height)
- 9 x 17 in. (23 x 23 cm) rectangle of cream canvas (width x height)
- Driftwood stick approximately 2 in. (5 cm) in circumference and 11 in. (28 cm) long
- Craft drill with 1/16 in. (1.5 mm) titanium-coated drill bit
- Small block of wood
- Six razor clam shells
- Long, slim, sewing needle
- Five small, flat pebbles and one small scallop shell
- Sewing machine
- Long, slim, embroidery needle

Techniques

- Preparing fabrics for embroidery, page 14
- Embroidery threads and yarns, page 15
- Blanket stitch, page 16
- Cross-Stitch, page 17

1 Set the machine to medium straight stitch and sew the 9 in. (23 cm) squares of cream and sand linen together along one edge, taking a ⅝ in. (1.5 cm) seam allowance. Press the seam open.

2 Press under a ½ in. (1 cm) hem on the two long edges of the 9 x 5½ in. (23 x 14 cm) rectangle of cream linen. Pin it to the sand-colored square, 1¼ in. (3 cm) above the join.

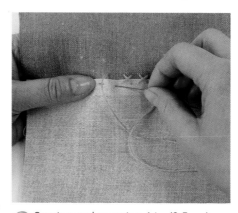

3 Starting and stopping 1 in. (2.5 cm) from either edge, embroider a line of cross-stitches in apricot floss along both long sides of the cream linen to attach it to the sand-colored square.

4 Pin the photograph to the cream-colored square, 1¼ in. (3 cm) below the seam line. Starting and stopping 1 in. (2.5 cm) from either edge, embroider a line of blanket stitches in vanilla floss along both long sides to attach it to the square.

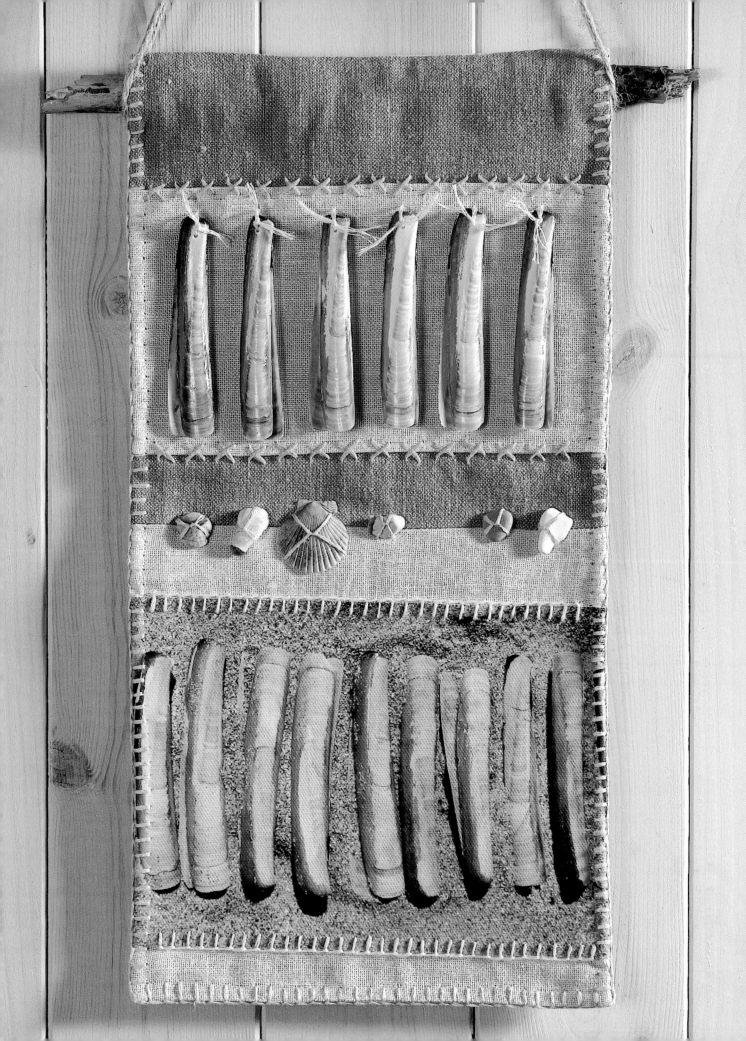

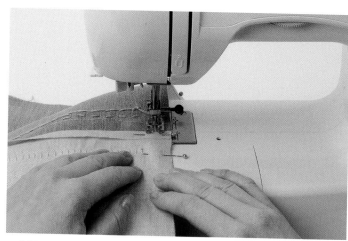

5 Right sides together, lay the embroidered linen rectangle over the cream canvas rectangle, aligning the raw edges. Pin the layers together around the edges. Machine stitch across the top edge, taking a ⅝ in. (1.5 cm) seam allowance.

6 Measure from the line of machine stitching and mark with a pin 1⅜ in. (3.5 cm) down the side. Machine stitch from the marked point to the bottom. Repeat on the other side.

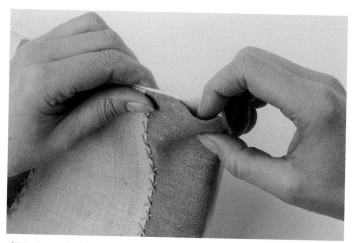

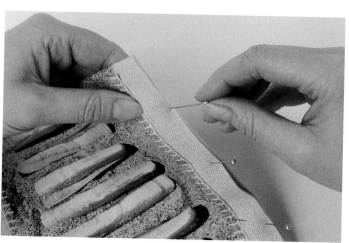

7 Through the bottom opening, turn the rectangles right side out. At the top corners (where the small openings are), make sure that the seam allowance is tucked in so that the sides of the wall hanging are straight.

8 Turn in the bottom edges ⅝ in. (1.5 cm) and pin them together.

sew**SMART**

Save the rest of each skein of embroidery thread you use in making this wall hanging, so you can change to new shells or found objects and create an entirely new look with a minimal amount of stitching.

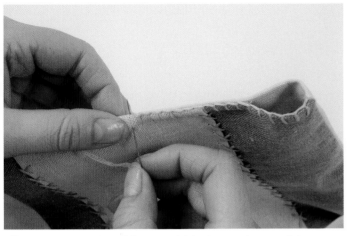 

9 Using stone-colored floss, work blanket stitch around three edges of the wall hanging. Start at the top of one side, work down the side, across the bottom, and up the other side.

10 At the top, stitch through the linen only, ensuring that the openings in the sides remain open. Thread the stick through the top of the wall hanging, so that it protrudes evenly on each side.

 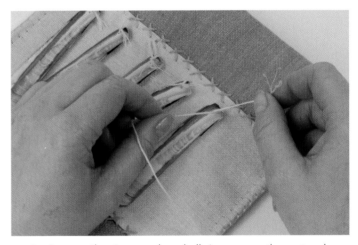

11 Lay one end of a razor clam shell on the small block of wood and, using the craft drill, drill a small hole through both halves of each shell, using consistent, gentle pressure.

12 Arrange the six razor clam shells in a row on the rectangle of cream linen. Stitch each one in place with vanilla floss. Take the long, slim needle down through the hole in the shell and through the fabric. Bring the needle back out just above the shell and tie the ends in a flat knot. Trim the thread ends to ⅝ in. (1.5 cm).

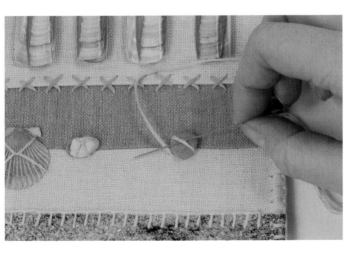

13 Arrange the pebbles and scallop shell across the seam stitched in Step 1. Stitch them in place through all layers of fabric. Make one diagonal stitch across the item. Bring the needle up through the fabric as if you were going to work the second half of a cross stitch. Take the needle under the first stitch, then down through the fabric to complete the stitch. Secure the thread on the back, then stitch on the next item, until all are in place.

Ideas Gallery hand embroidery

Colorful threads worked with artful embroidery stitches transform ordinary fabric designs into fashion statements. Refer to pages 16–19 to see how to work them.

➤ **The existing overcheck** of this herringbone tweed is echoed with an overcheck worked in cross-stitch.

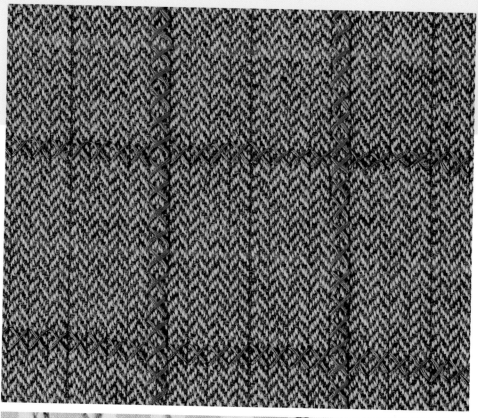

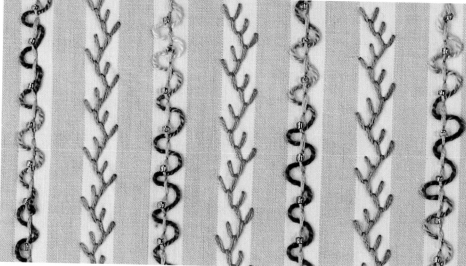

◄ **Raised satin stitches,** worked in stranded embroidery floss, cover the berries on this printed fabric and give a dimensional quality to the cloth.

⋀ **Alternate rows of double-feather stitch** and threaded backstitch are worked along the stripes of this cotton fabric. The backstitch incorporates seed beads, and the striped fabric helps to keep the stitching even.

◄ **Printed cloth** with backstitches worked in stranded embroidery floss. Some of the floral motifs are decorated with flower sequins and secured with French knots.

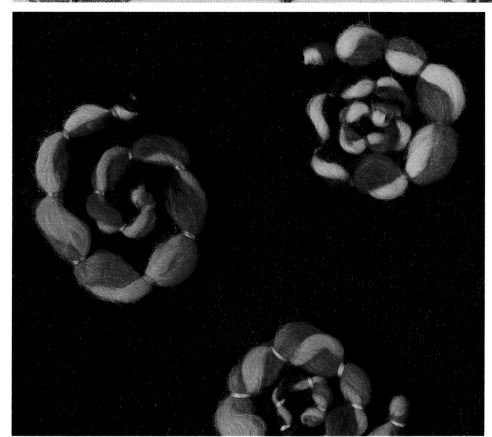

▼ **Purchased flower braid trimmings** can be cut up to provide individual decorative motifs. They are scattered in between detached chain stitches worked into lazy daisies and secured with French knots.

▲ **Uneven variegated, chunky yarn** is curled into spirals and stabilized with stranded embroidery floss. A knot at either end of the wool spiral prevents the wool from pulling out of the stitching.

Machine embroidery

Machine embroidery can be a quick way of adding decorative detail and extra interest to an original project or purchased item. All but the most basic sewing machines feature a number of preset embroidery stitches. Free-motion machine embroidery offers vast creative potential: Your sewing machine becomes a freehand drawing tool.

Using the sewing machine

Most machines can be used to great effect in machine embroidery, especially when it comes to border or edging treatments. Free-motion embroidery requires the teeth in the throat plate (the feed dogs) to be lowered, so the work can be moved around under the needle in any direction. It's best to use a special foot (generally purchased separately) that sits just above the surface of the fabric. Machine embroidery can be used on light- to mediumweight fabrics; some machines may not be able to cope with heavyweight ones. Remember to change the sewing machine needle to suit the type of fabric you are stitching. Always consult your sewing machine manual for specific advice on your machine, and be sure to test each decorative embroidery stitch to establish the optimum settings before you begin.

Using a hoop

It's best to use a hoop for machine embroidery. Insert the fabric into the hoop the opposite way to hand embroidery—with the inner ring facing upward so that the fabric will lie flat on the bed of the sewing machine. The right side of the fabric is uppermost, as the decorative thread is on the top spool of the sewing machine. If the decorative thread is wound onto the bobbin, as opposed to the top spool, the fabric would need to be the other way up in the hoop. Hoops sold especially for machine embroidery are shallower than those used for hand embroidery; this allows them to slip easily under the presser foot of the sewing machine.

Machine-embroidery threads

Any general-purpose sewing thread can be used for machine embroidery, but threads produced especially for this purpose tend to be finer. There are many types available, including metallic, iridescent, variegated, and high luster threads (see below). It is best to work with a thicker needle, such as a size 90, when using fine embroidery thread. This offers greater protection for the thread as it passes through the fabric and helps to prevent it from snapping. Texture can be added by working with thicker threads, such as fine wools and metallic braids. These can be wound onto the bobbin. You may have to adjust the tension and you will have to work with the wrong side of the fabric facing up. Many of the specialty embroidery threads can be blended to create lustrous color combinations and unique variations in texture.

Keep the fabric taut in a hoop as you stitch for best results.

A range of machine embroidery threads, left to right:

- Polyester
- Rayon
- Two-color rayon
- Variegated viscose
- Silk

- Metallic-effect synthetic fiber
- Metallic-effect polyester
- Variegated metallic
- Metallic
- Holographic

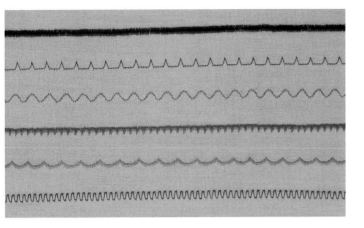

Using decorative stitches

Preset embroidery stitches can be made to look different by changing the stitch width and stitch length, so take time to experiment to get the best effect. Use decorative stitches to add a special touch to plain household linens, for example. Although some, such as the blind hemming stitch have other applications, they can be used to good effect as decorative stitches in their own right.

Top to bottom
Satin stitch, blind hemming stitch, stepped scallop stitch, two-width satin stitch, scallop stitch, and box stitch.

Free-motion machine embroidery

The free-motion technique can be used to fill in details on a background, or to make a surface composed entirely of stitches. Straight stitch or zigzag stitch can be used. Simply place the hoop under the sewing machine needle, lower the feed dogs then lower the darning foot onto the fabric. Hold the hoop on both sides and move it with your fingers, allowing your fingers to move as necessary, but keeping the sides of your hands on the machine bed for stability.

Embroidering on water-soluble fabric

Machine stitching on water-soluble fabric is a fun way of creating lace-effect fabrics or motifs. How thoroughly you rinse the fabric after embroidering will affect the finish of the piece. Fabric soaked for a short time will retain a residue—providing stiffness and allowing it to be molded into shapes. This can be useful when creating sculptural pieces that will not be washed. Place the water-soluble fabric in an embroidery hoop and embroider it in the usual way. If you are creating lace effects, be sure that all the individual motifs are linked or the fabric will fall apart when the material is dissolved away.

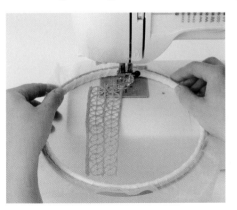

1 Lacy effects can easily be created by embroidering onto water-soluble fabric. Using the free-motion embroidery technique shown above, embroider a design onto the soluble fabric.

2 Using sharp scissors, cut away any excess fabric around the embroidery.

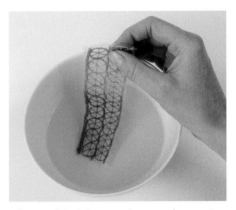

3 Carefully following the manufacturer's instructions, dip the embroidery into cold water. The longer you leave the piece in the water, the more fabric will dissolve and the softer the end result will be. Let the embroidery dry on a flat surface.

Flower pin

This beautiful bloom is deceptively easy to create! Worked in machine embroidery using water-soluble fabric, which is later dissolved, the petals are left stiff enough to retain a realistic form. This budding flower can easily be transformed into a corsage with a satin ribbon or into a barette with a metal clasp.

Materials

- 10 x 10 in. (25 x 25 cm) square of medium-weight, white, man-made-fiber fabric
- 10 x 10 in. (25 x 25 cm) square of water-soluble fabric
- Embroidery hoop
- Template on page 156
- Water-erasable marking pen
- Long hand-sewing needle
- Size 90 machine needle
- Cream, light purple, and dark purple rayon machine embroidery threads
- Bowl of water
- Small square of short-pile, wine-red velvet
- 28-gauge silver wire
- Plum-colored delica beads
- Silver and opalescent fire-polished beads
- ¾ in. (18 mm) metal self-cover button
- Small pliers
- Epoxy adhesive
- Pin back
- Sewing machine

Techniques

- Embroidery threads, page 15
- Using a hoop, page 28
- Free-motion machine embroidery, page 29
- Embroidering on water-soluble fabric, page 29
- Covering buttons, page 142

1 Lay the white fabric on top of the water-soluble fabric with right side up and tighten them in the embroidery hoop. Photocopy the template, cut it out, and trace around it onto the white fabric with a water-erasable marking pen.

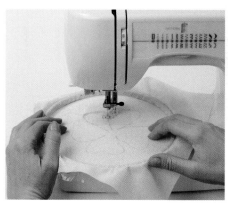

2 Set the machine up for free-motion machine embroidery using a straight stitch and a size 90 machine needle. Thread the machine with cream thread. Outline each petal in a broad band of stitches at top edge and narrowing it down each side.

3 Thread the machine with the light purple thread and start to fill in the petals. Leave a space between the cream and purple stitching. Stitch in a fan shape to emphasize the shape of the petals, and do not make the top edge of the stitching too solid.

4 Change the thread in the machine to dark purple thread and embroider the inner part of each petal in the same way, echoing the fan shape of the outer area so embroidery is concentrated around the center of the flower.

5 Cut out the flower very carefully. Cut as close as possible to the embroidery without cutting any stitches.

6 Dip the flower into water to dissolve the soluble fabric and remove any pen marks. Do not soak the embroidery in the water: The flower will benefit from the stiffness created by the residue of the soluble fabric remaining in the stitching. Arrange the petals into pleasing shapes and leave the flower on a towel to dry.

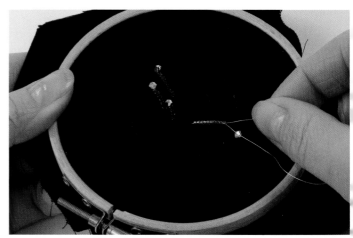

7 Insert the velvet into the embroidery hoop. Trace around the cutting-out template of the button, then place the button itself in the middle of this circle and trace around it. Working within the small circle, make the wired stamens. Arrange them in an outer circle of eight, an inner circle of six, and one central one. Use the needle to pierce a hole in the fabric, then push the end of each wire through from back to front. Leave a 2 in. (5 cm) end at the back; cut, then bend it flat against the fabric while you are working.

8 Thread on nine to fourteen beads and either a silver or opalescent crystal. Skipping the crystal, take the wire back down through the beads and fabric, as shown above. Repeat to make each stamen, varying the number of beads and alternating the color of the crystal. Secure the stamens by twisting the wires together and trimming them as necessary on the back of the work.

9 Use the pliers to pull the shank out of the top of the button. Cut out the fabric around the traced line for the button cover and gather the edge. Cover the button top, pull, and tie off the gathering thread, but do not snap on the back of the button.

10 Using doubled thread, stitch the button into the center of the flower. Bring the needle up through the flower, then through the velvet on the very edge of the button. Take it back down through the flower again and repeat all around the edge of the button.

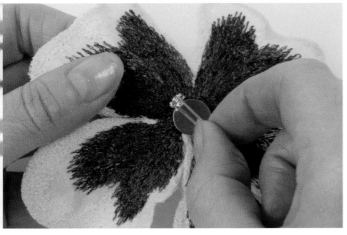

11 To make the flower into a brooch, glue a pin back to the very center of the flower back.

Designing with threads

Rayon and polyester threads Rayon threads are very lustrous and ideal for designs that call for areas of high sheen. Polyester threads are also shiny, but less so than their rayon counterparts. Because polyester resists heat and rough treatment better than other fibers, it makes a solid choice for embroidering jeans or children's clothing.

Cotton and linen threads The color choice in cotton threads is limited, but cotton still sets the standard for hand-quilted designs, and linen does the same for hand-drawn embroidery techniques worked on 100 percent linen fabrics. If you are looking for a specific color, you can probably find it easily through the Internet.

Silk thread and silk-ribbon embroidery thread Natural silk fibers are dyed and spun to make beautiful, vibrant, durable threads. They are ideal for hand-sewn crewel and needlepoint designs, especially for rendering small details, since their sheen makes them eye-catching.

Novelty threads Almost any thin string, cord, or raffia for example, can be used as a thread for a particular design effect. Metallic machine-embroidery thread has a polyester-filament core for strength and ease, while other metallic threads are twisted into fine braids.

Ideas Gallery machine embroidery

These days sewing machines offer a variety of creative embroidery techniques. Use built-in stitches alone or in combinations to create visually arresting effects that you can add to your clothing or home furnishings.

➤ **Multicolored rayon** machine-embroidery thread and a decorative stitch were used to create a lattice effect between the floral sprigs on this printed cotton. The thread subtly changes color, adding visual interest.

▼ **Stepped satin stitch**, in alternate rows of green and ivory, was used to apply gingham bias binding to this cotton fabric. The stripes were further embellished with evenly-spaced matching buttons.

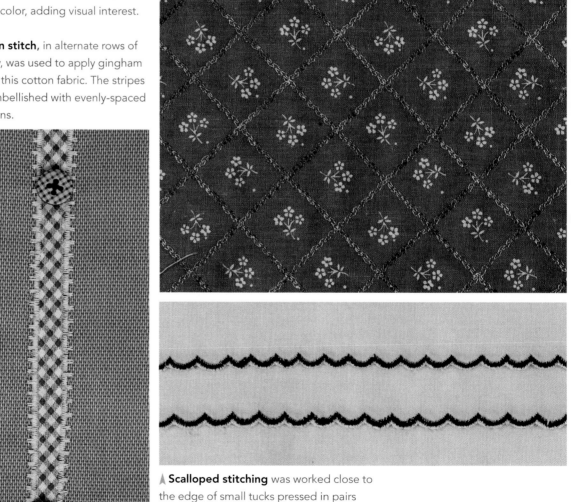

⋀ **Scalloped stitching** was worked close to the edge of small tucks pressed in pairs into this lightweight cotton fabric. The fabric next to the fold was then cut away close to the stitching to create tucks with scalloped edges.

◄ **Ordinary machine thread** was used to sew lines of wavy stitching at either side of alternate green stripes in this fabric. The same stitch in a contrasting color runs down the center of the stitch-decorated stripes, with two lines overlaid to create an interlaced effect. The striped fabric serves as a guide to keep the lines of stitching straight.

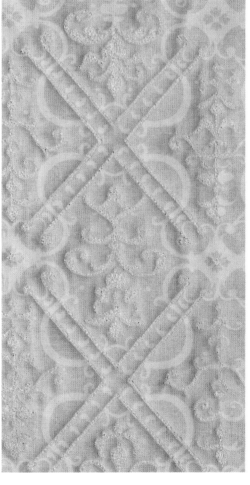

◢ **Straight stitch** is used to draw loose flower images onto fabric. Subtle coloring is added by dampening sections of the cloth and brushing on water-based fabric dyes, which bleed across the wet areas. Follow the manufacturers instructions for setting the dye.

◄ **The design** of a printed fabric can provide a base for machine embroidery. This fabric has been layered with cotton batting and a fabric lining and the lattice and other elements of the design were embroidered in self-color thread, using straight stitches to create a unique quilted effect.

Appliqué

While hand appliqué is a traditional quiltmaking technique, modern decorative machine stitches allow you to interpret this technique in a whole new way and make the process go much faster. Both methods can be simplified by using fusible webbing to bond motifs to a background fabric and then outlining them with decorative stitching.

You'll enjoy using appliqué to accessorize a garment artfully, brighten up your home decor with charming accessories, or even transform a nursery into an imaginary world that will delight any child.

Hand appliqué

Traditional appliqué has a very distinctive appearance, each shape having a slightly padded edge. Different types of appliqué have evolved in different parts of the world, each reflecting the styles of clothing and the look of the surroundings in that area of the world. Using the glorious array of fabrics available today, you can create appliqué designs that reflect your own color preferences and sense of personal style.

Preparing fabrics

It is not necessary to buy expensive fabrics for appliqué, your scrap bag can yield some exciting finds. Think carefully about color, texture, and shape—try to experiment with unusual color combinations. Though it is possible to sew almost any two types of fabric together, the most successful and durable results are achieved when you match materials of similar weights. Background fabrics should ideally have a firm, close weave and be strong enough to support the additional layers of appliqué shapes. If the piece will not be subjected to much wear and tear or heavy laundering, delicate, lightweight fabrics can yield some exciting results. If the piece will require frequent laundering, choose medium-weight cottons and wash and press the fabrics before using them.

sewSMART

For times when you want to "fussy out" appliqué shapes to highlight a decorative element, try cutting a "window" template of the shape you want to stitch. Draw or trace the finished shape onto paper and cut out exactly on the marked line, leaving a "window" in the desired shape. Place the paper on the fabric and when you are pleased with the way it looks, mark inside the lines of the "window." Remove the paper and cut the shape with a ³⁄₁₆ in. (4.5 mm) seam allowance.

Using patterned fabrics

Individual motifs can be cut out from strongly patterned fabrics, such as bold floral prints, or other decorative fabrics. Results range from fun and whimsical to rich and opulent, depending on your preferences.

This little bird has been cut out from a fabric with an all-over repeat design. Appliqué is an ideal technique for making coordinating accessories for a child's room.

Bold floral motifs are good subjects for hand appliqué. Rearrange them into a new design of your own.

Strips and larger sections of printed fabric can also be used, as well as smaller motifs.

Making templates

Appliqué patterns are drawn to finished size on your template material. The seam allowance is added on later by eye, as each shape is cut from fabric. For a shape that will only be used once, a paper shape can be cut out and used as a pattern. If the motif is to be used several times, make a more durable template by transferring the shape onto thin cardboard or template plastic and cutting around it. When working with complex layered appliqué, trace the individual shapes separately, labeling each one carefully.

Using paper

This is a simple way of transferring a chosen motif onto fabric for hand appliqué. Photocopy, trace, or draw the appliqué motif onto plain paper and cut it out as shown right, to make a template. Pin the template to the fabric and cut out shape.

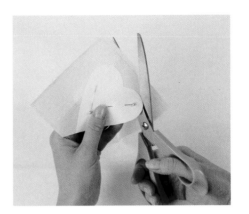

Using cardboard or plastic templates

Use this technique if you are marking several identical motifs. If you plan to use the template repeatedly, it's better to cut it out of cardboard or template plastic. If you are using fusible web, iron it onto the fabric, then lay the template on the paper side and mark around it as many times as required, leaving a seam allowance if necessary.

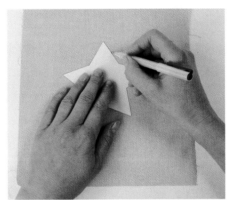

sewSMART

In the case of letters, numbers, or other such one-way designs, remember that you must reverse the template before you mark around it on the fabric.

Marking with a carbon pencil

If the motif you want to appliqué is complex, or has internal details you want to embroider, you can transfer it onto fabric using a carbon pencil.

1 If you are using fusible web, iron it onto the back of the fabric. Lay a sheet of thin plain paper over the printed motif. Trace over the lines with a carbon pencil.

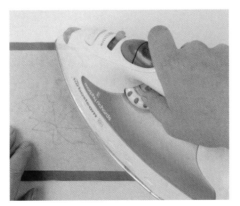

2 Lay the paper on the right side of the fabric with the carbon lines face down. Iron the back of the paper to transfer the lines onto the fabric. Lift off the paper to reveal the marked appliqué motif.

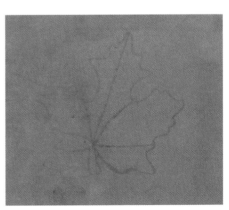

3 Carbon lines show up well on most fabrics. If they are a little faint, you can go over them with another fabric-marking pen or pencil.

Using Fusible Web

Using fusible web will prevent fabrics from fraying and is a quick-and-easy method of preparing a motif for hand appliqué. Cut a piece of fusible web that is slightly smaller than your appliqué fabric, and follow these steps.

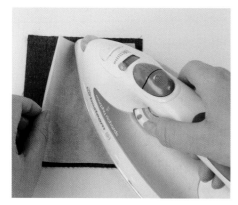

1 Lay the fusible web paper side up on the wrong side of the appliqué fabric and, carefully following the manufacturer's instructions, press it onto the fabric.

2 Mark the appliqué shape on the paper surface of the fusible web and carefully cut it out.

3 Peel the paper backing from the fusible web.

4 Lay the appliqué motif face up on the right side of the background fabric and press it in position.

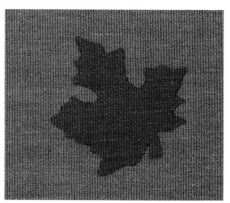

5 After the motif is firmly bonded to the fabric, stitch around it using one of the embroidery stitches on pages 16–19.

sewSMART

Be careful to place your appliqué paper side up on the fabric or it will promptly stick to the bottom of the iron. It is good practice to stitch around the edge of the motif after it has been applied; this can be done in a variety of ways either by hand or machine.

Traditional turned-edge appliqué

Place each template on the right side of the appropriate fabric and mark around it. Cut out each shape ¼ in. (5 mm) outside the marked lines and stitch them to the background fabrics following the steps below.

1 Turn under ¼ in. (5 mm) along one edge. Knot one end to anchor thread. Baste along folded edge.

2 At a corner, fold over the point to the depth of the folded seam allowance. Turn under the edges on either side to miter the corner seam allowance.

3 Baste over the mitered point and along the next side of the shape. The motif is now ready to be stitched to the background fabric.

Taming peaks and valleys

On a motif such as a star, each peak is an outer point and each valley is an inner point.

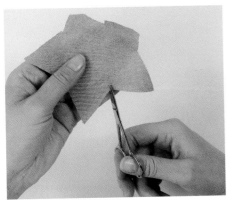

1 At a valley, snip into the fabric up to, but not through, the marked line.

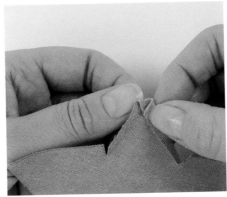

2 Use your fingers to press under a ¼ in. (5 mm) seam allowance from valley to peak; fold the peak over into a neat point.

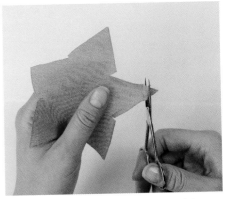

3 To reduce bulk, cut off the tip of the peak, within the folded-over seam allowance.

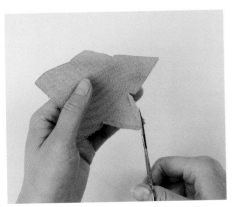

4 Also to reduce bulk, trim just a little fabric from the folded-over seam allowance on either side of the peak.

5 Fold the seam allowances over the peak and baste them carefully in place.

6 Treat the peaks and valleys carefully for best results when you stitch the shape to the background fabric.

Clipping curves
Follow the steps to prepare smooth curved edges for hand appliqué.

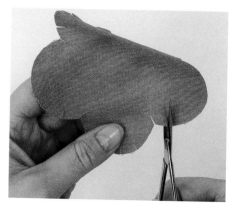

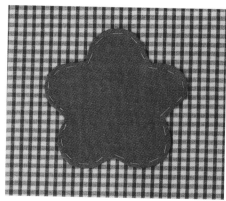

1 Use sharp scissors to clip at close intervals along the curve, cutting to the depth of the seam allowance. The tighter the curve, the more frequently it needs to be clipped to produce a neat turned edge. Clip into any valleys.

2 Start basting the seam allowance along the curve. Fold it under as you go, keeping the curve neat and smooth and allowing the clipped sections on the back to overlap as they wish.

3 Careful clipping and basting will enable you to stitch smooth curves when you appliqué each shape to the background fabric.

Blind stitching
For traditional hand appliqué, anchor shapes using blind stitch.

1 Thread a sewing needle with thread that matches the color of the appliqué shape and knot one end. Bring the needle through the background fabric and shape, as close to the edge of the shape as possible. Take the needle down through the background fabric, close to where it came up. Bring the tip of the needle back through the background fabric about ⅛ in. (3 mm) farther along the edge of the fold, catching the fold of the appliqué shape with the tip of the needle. Pull the thread all the way through.

2 Take the needle back down through the background fabric to begin another stitch. Repeat this process and continue stitching until the whole motif is stitched in place. Using the tips of the blades of a small pair of scissors, snip and pull out the basting stitches around the edge of the motif.

Embellishments

You can enhance hand appliqué with beads and ribbons, buttons, sequins, and more. Explore the potential in some of the following ideas and create your own designs.

Hand embroidery

On turned-edge appliqué, embroidery can be used to secure motifs in place. Embroidery stitches can be worked in matching thread for a subtle effect, or in a contrasting color to draw more attention to the motif. They can be used effectively for outlining, edging, and filling. Outlining stitches, such as backstitch, can also hold motifs in place, as well as add ornament; edging stitches, such as blanket stitch, can mask the join between two fabrics, and some stitches, such as French knots, add texture.

Left to right: backstitch, cross-stitch, chain stitch, blanket stitch, couching (all stems are backstitched).

Baubles, bangles, and beads

The addition of embellishments can add an extra dimension to hand appliqué, and there are literally hundreds to choose from. Have fun selecting from the vast range of sequins, beads, buttons, ribbons, and so on to find the perfect finishing touches for your projects.

Satin ribbon

Embroidered patch and fabric trim

Sequins

Seed beads

Bugle beads

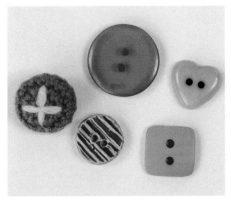

Shaped buttons

Summer hat

Hand appliqué can often be simple in style, but here the muted palette and elegant foliage create a sophisticated look. Apply the motifs and embroider around the edges. Although fusible webbing is a more modern invention, the hand embroidered finish lends a traditional decoration.

Materials

- Fabric hat with a straight crown and a wide brim
- Striped fabric
- Fusible interfacing
- ½ in. (1 cm)-wide ribbon to match the hat
- Stranded cotton embroidery floss in two colors, one to complement the striped fabric and one to match the hat
- Embroidery needle
- Fusible web
- Fabric with distinct motif
- Eight buttons
- ¼ in. (5 mm)-wide silk ribbon

Techniques

- Coral stitch, page 18
- Using patterned fabrics, page 38
- Fusible web, page 40
- Hand embroidery, page 43

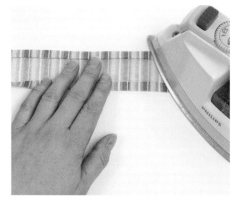

1 Cut a strip of striped fabric measuring 2⅝ in. (6.5 cm) by the circumference of the hat plus 1¼ in. (3 cm). The stripes should run across the fabric. Cut a strip of fusible interfacing to the same size and iron it onto the back of the fabric. Press under ½ in. (1 cm) along each long edge.

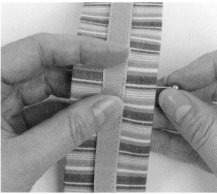

2 Cut the ½ in. (1 cm)-wide ribbon to the same length as the the fabric. Pin the ribbon along the center of the fabric. Thread the sewing machine and set it to a medium straight stitch. Sew the ribbon to the center of the fabric, stitching both sides close to the edge.

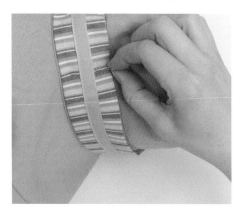

3 Pin the ends of the fabric together. Check that the band fits the crown of the hat, then sew the ends together, taking a ⅝ in. (1.5 cm) seam. Press. Match the back seam of the band and the back of the hat, and pin the band in place.

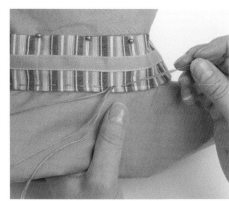

4 Thread the embroidery needle with the floss that complements the striped fabric and tie a knot in one end. Using running stitch and working ¼ in. (5 mm) in from the edges, sew the band to the hat.

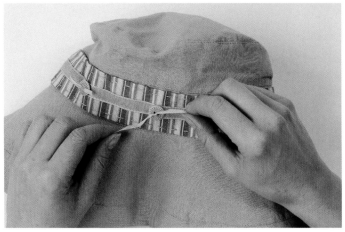

5 Evenly space the eight buttons around the hat and mark their positions with pins. Thread the embroidery needle with the silk ribbon. Pass the needle through the button and through the hat at the marked point, and out again a little distance away. Pass the needle through the other hole of the button from back to front. Pull the ribbon through and cut it, so that there is a 2½ in. (6 cm) tail of ribbon emerging from each hole. Tie a firm double knot and trim the ends at a slant.

6 Iron the fusible web onto the back of the patterned fabric. Carefully cut out sections of pattern.

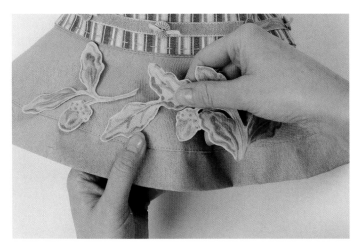

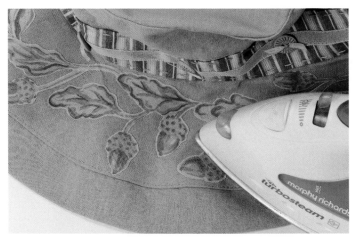

7 Arrange the motifs around the brim of the hat. If the pattern permits, consider overlapping pieces to produce one continuous motif that runs around the brim.

8 As you complete a section of the arrangement, iron the motifs in place.

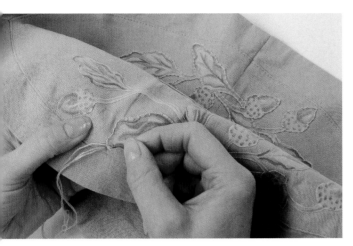 

9 Iron a motif to the underside of the brim at the back, so that when the brim is turned up, it shows. Using the floss that matches the hat, embroider around the edges of the appliqué shapes, using coral stitch. Make sure that your stitches do not show on the upper side of the brim.

10 Using the same technique, embroider around the edges of the appliqué shape on the top of the brim. Make sure that your stitches do not show on the underside of the brim.

sewSMART

Consider using any leftover pieces of the patterned fabric to cut more appliqué shapes; stitch these onto a tote bag or the ends of a simple scarf to create a coordinated accessory to go with the hat.

Ideas Gallery hand appliqué

From folk art to vintage laces to recycled clothing, the inspirations for hand appliqué are limitless.

➤ **Fusible web** is a means of adhering one fabric to another, but it also helps to prevent raw edges from fraying. If the piece is only going to receive light wear, it is possible to leave the edges unstitched. This little rabbit sits on a background of linen embellished with cross-stitch. A piece of checked ribbon secured with straight stitches forms a border. Buttons, a tiny bead, and a small pompom add further detail.

◄ **Get the effect of glass** or transparent objects by overlaying with organza. Cut out flowers and attach to ground, adding embroidered stems. Draw a vase onto the cloth using a fabric marker. Pin a piece of organza over the area and stitch in place with satin stitch.

▲ **A diamond of fabric** cut from another contrasting coordinated print have been applied to the printed diamond shapes on this fabric, using fusible web. Coral stitch has been worked around the edge of the appliqué shape, using variegated hand-dyed, stranded floss.

◄ **A variety of embroidery** stitches can be used in one project. Felt circles backed with fusible web are ironed onto fabric, with a lace border applied with zigzag stitch. The circles have a chain stitch or spiral of running stitch decoration.

⋀ **Use embellishments** to add texture and dimension. This simple bird boasts real feathers for his wing and tail. The bird is cut from patterned cloth backed with fusible web and is ironed onto a calico that features pinked edges. Outline the bird with running stitch, use satin stitch to make the beak and embroider some feet. Sew on a sequin eye and attach the patch to a coordinating piece of patterned fabric, using running stitch. Secure the feathers with a few stitches.

◄ **Give a motif a padded effect** and add a relief quality by layering it with cotton batting. Cut a piece of cotton batting the same size as the motif. Leaving a seam allowance around the edge of the motif, pin it to the background fabric, sandwiching the batting between the layers. Sew around the motif. Trim the seam allowance close to the stitching. Using stranded floss, pick out details on the motif with backstitch.

Machine appliqué

Machine stitching can be used to attach motifs cut from many different types of fabrics, including ones that do not fray. It's a great finishing technique for bonded motifs, providing a flat, durable result.

Straight stitch

Straight stitch can be used for machine appliquéing fabrics that do not fray and where the cut edges do not need to be hidden. Set the stitch length on your sewing machine slightly shorter than for piecing. Stitch inside the edge of the appliqué (motif) using the edge of the presser foot as your guide.

Satin stitch

Satin stitch is a dense zigzag stitch that provides good coverage. It has a lovely braid like look when worked correctly, in either standard sewing thread or embroidery thread. Set your machine to sew a wide zigzag stitch, and close the stitch length until the stitches are formed very closely together. Work slowly and carefully, manipulating the fabric through the machine, so that the presser foot is parallel to the edge. Some machines are supplied with a special appliqué foot, which makes it much easier to follow the needle as you sew. If necessary, you can also use an embroidery hoop to help prevent your work from distorting while you are stitching.

Right-angled corners

The neatest way of working a right-angle corner is to reposition the needle rather than stitching over an existing line of stitches, which will almost certainly create a very bulky corner.

1 Sew right up to the corner, ending the line of stitching with the needle down in the fabric on the outside edge of the satin stitching. Lift the presser foot and rotate the fabric around the needle, ready to sew the next line of stitching.

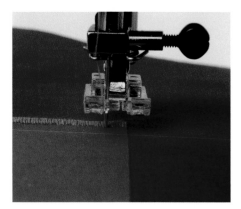

2 Lower the foot and lift the needle from the fabric. Lift the foot and carefully slide the fabric back under the foot until the needle is in line with the bottom edge of the previous line of stitching. Manually turn the wheel of the machine until the needle moves to the left and drops down through the fabric, continue stitching.

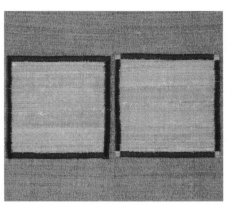

3 The motif on the left has perfectly satin-stitched corners, while the corners on the right-hand motif are badly worked, resulting in an untidy finish.

Using tear-away stabilizer

Lightweight fabrics can become distorted during the sewing process. This can be resolved with additional support. It may not always be appropriate to use fusible interlining or an additional layer of fabric, so a good solution is to use a layer of stabilizing material, which can simply be torn away when the stitching is complete. Although a special tearaway material is available in fabric and craft stores, thin paper, such as dressmakers' pattern paper or artists' layout paper, can also work as well. To use this technique, follow these steps:

1 Lay the background fabric on top of a sheet of stabilizer. Pin the layers together through the background fabric.

2 Machine appliqué the motif to the background with satin stitch, sewing through all layers.

3 On the back, carefully tear away the paper inside and outside the stitching.

4 Press the finished appliqué shape and background fabric.

sewSMART

A neat, tapered look can be achieved at corners by varying the stitch width as you approach the corner. Most machines will enable you to adjust the stitch width. Simply decrease the stitch width as you approach the corner; then pivot the work, and increase the stitch width slowly as you move away from the corner.

Reverse appliqué

Reverse appliqué involves cutting into layers of fabric, rather than patching them on. In this type of machine appliqué, the design is created by cutting away areas of the top fabrics to reveal the colors underneath. Traditionally, the edges of the cut fabric are turned under and hand stitched, but machine satin stitch can be used to outline shapes quickly, and prevent edges from fraying.

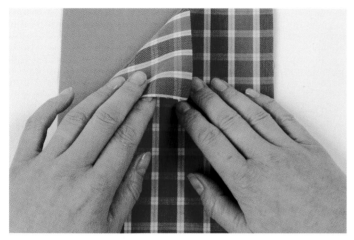

1 Lay the piece of fabric that will form the background (top) over the piece that will form the appliqué motif.

2 Mark the appliqué motif onto the background (top) piece of fabric. Pin the layers of fabric together.

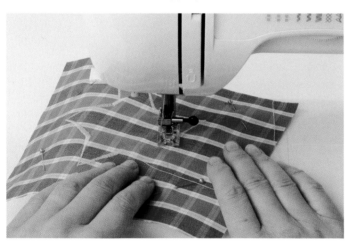

3 Using satin stitch and tapering the corners, machine stitch along the marked lines of the motif.

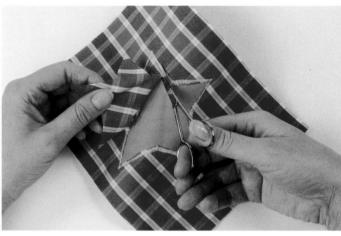

4 Make a small cut with a pair of scissors, and very carefully, without cutting the bottom layer of fabric or the stitching, cut away the top layer of fabric, allowing the underneath fabric to take the shape of the appliqué motif. Iron the motif.

sewSMART

Most sewing machines feature a variety of preset embroidery stitches, and they make lovely edgings for appliqué motifs. When making your selection, consider whether you wish to completely conceal the edges of the motif beneath your stitching, or let them remain visible.

Satin-stitched bed linens

Embellishing long, straight edges, such as those on bed linens can add a stylish touch to your bedroom decor. Choose fabrics and colors to complement your bedroom furnishings, and decorate your bed linens with simple techniques, such as machine embroidery or machine appliqué. In this project, a form of reverse appliqué has been used, with the top fabric cut away to reveal a complementary color below.

Materials

- Thin paper for pattern
- Carbon pencil
- Sheet
- Strip of contrast-color fabric in the width of the sheet by 8 in. (20 cm) deep.
- Basting thread
- Two colors of sewing thread to complement the fabrics
- Air-erasable fabric marker
- Pillowcase with border

Techniques

- Using a carbon pencil, page 39
- Using the sewing machine, page 28
- Right-angled corners, page 50
- Decorative stitches, page 50
- Reverse appliqué, page 52

sewSMART

If your sheet won't fit evenly with whole pattern repeats, don't worry; just place the design centrally on the sheet, so there is the same amount of part repeat at either side. Draw over all the lines of the pattern with the carbon pencil, then continue as normal.

1 Using the carbon pencil, create a template onto the thin paper, repeating it as many times as necessary to make a pattern wide enough to fit across the top edge of your sheet.

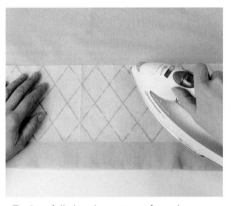

2 Carefully lay the pattern face down across the top of the sheet on the right side, butting one edge against the stitched hemline. Iron the back of the paper to transfer the lines onto the sheet.

3 Lay the contrast fabric behind the area of the sheet covered by the pattern. Position it centrally and, working on the right side, pin the layers together.

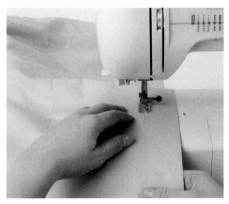

4 Set your sewing machine to the longest straight stitch and baste the layers together along both the top and bottom edges.

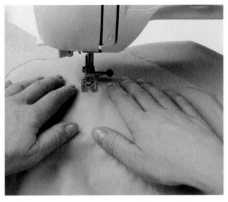

5 Thread the sewing machine with one of the colored threads and set a wide satin stitch. Starting at the top left of the pattern, stitch down the first diagonal line, between the lines of basting.

6 At the bottom, where two lines join, turn the fabric with the needle down and stitch up the adjoining line. Continue stitching a zigzag pattern all the way across the sheet. Repeat in the opposite direction to form large stitched diamonds.

7 Carefully cut away the top fabric within the diamonds to reveal the contrast fabric beneath. Cut as close as possible to the stitching, being very careful to not cut into it.

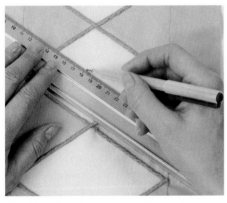

8 Now that the contrast diamonds are exposed, lay the ruler across each diamond, and line the ends up with the ends of the lines on the background fabric. Use fabric marker to re-draw the lines.

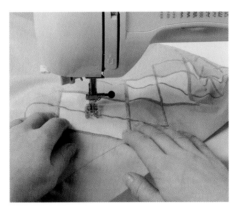

9 Thread the sewing machine with the other color thread. Set to a narrow satin stitch and stitch over the lines, across the diamonds and over the previous lines of stitching where the new lines cross them.

10 Thread the machine with the first color thread and set it to the wide satin stitch. Stitch over basting lines at the top and bottom of the pattern, while stitching over the ends of the zigzags. At the beginning and end of the pattern— next to the edges of the sheet—stitch lines close to the first and last diamonds, stitching the backing fabric to the main fabric.

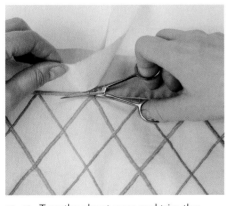

11 Turn the sheet over and trim the excess contrast color fabric outside the lines of stitching done in Step 10.

12 Draw lines across the pillowcase border from the stitching to the corner. Using the widest satin stitch, stitch over the existing stitched lines. Run stitches to the edge of the pillowcase at each corner.

Child's jumper

Bold and vibrant appliqués make an ideal embellishment for children's clothing and kids love the colorful results! A lively fantasy landscape decorates this smart denim jumper. Some elements are attached with parts remaining free to add a tactile and dimensional quality to the motifs. The color scheme was inspired by the striped top purchased to wear with the jumper. This can be a clever way to coordinate the child's outfit.

Materials

- Templates on page 156
- 2 ⅞ in. (7 cm)-square of green fabric backed with fusible web
- 4 x 2 ⅞ in. (10 x 7 cm)-piece of sparkly green fabric backed with fusible web
- 2 ⅞ in. (6 cm)-square of purple fabric backed with fusible web
- Scraps of turquoise, gold, pink, and plum satin backed with fusible web
- Two 10 x 10 in. (25 x 25 cm) pieces of pink shiny fabric
- 10 x 10 in. (25 x 25 cm) of white and gray organza; silver net; shot thin lilac fabric
- 8 in. (20 cm) embroidery hoop
- Size 90 sewing needle
- Assortment of embroidery threads and colored sequins
- Pale gray embroidery floss
- Two pink shisha mirrors
- Two ladybug buttons
- Air-erasable fabric marker
- Child's denim jumper

Techniques

- Using a hoop, page 28
- Embroidery threads, page 28
- Free-motion machine embroidery, page 29
- Satin stitch, page 50
- Right-angled corners, page 50
- Embroidery stitches, pages 16–19

1 Photocopy the templates and cut them out to make paper patterns. Cut two leaves from the matte green fabric and three from the sparkly green. Cut one pink leaf and two purple leaves. Cut out two flower centers from the turquoise fabric. Cut one bee body from the gold fabric and two butterfly bodies from the plum fabric.

2 Insert two layers of pink shiny fabric into the embroidery hoop. Draw around the flower pattern onto the top layer, fitting two flowers within the hoop. Using dark red thread, satin stitch around the edges, then work freehand petals in straight stitch, using this photograph as a guide. Cut out the flowers.

3 Sandwich a layer of white organza between two layers of gray organza and insert into the embroidery hoop. Trace bee wing pattern onto top layer. Using silver thread, outline the wings with several rows of straight stitch. Work shapes within the outline as shown here. Cut out the wings.

4 Sandwich a layer of silver net between a layer of gray organza and lilac fabric, and insert into the embroidery hoop. On gray side, trace the large wing pattern and embroider as shown. Turning the hoop and working on the lilac side, trace the lower wing pattern and embroider as shown.

5 Insert two layers of turquoise satin into the embroidery hoop and draw around the small butterfly wing pattern onto the top layer. Outline the wings in straight stitch then fill in the design with turquoise, green, and metallic green threads, using this photograph as a guide.

6 Arrange the elements of the front of the jumper (see photo). Draw around the elements with the air-erasable fabric marker. Also draw in the flower stems. After all their positions are established, remove the elements so that you can attach them individually.

7 First, use the iron to fuse all the green leaves onto the jumper as shown. Arrange the pink and purple leaves to make a flower and fuse them in place.

8 Using red thread, satin stitch around the flower petals. Using variegated green thread, stitch around the leaves and work the lines for the stems.

9 Using the same green thread and straight stitch, work some freehand lines on the green leaves to indicate their veins. In the same way, embroider a few blades of grass coming up from the hem of the jumper.

10 Use the iron to fuse the turquoise flower centers into the middle of the flowers. Position the flowers on the jumper. Using turquoise thread, satin stitch around the edge of the flower centers, attaching the flowers to the jumper.

sewSMART

If necessary, use the special tearaway stabilizing material as shown on page 51 when you stitch these shapes.

11 Position the bee's wings on the jumper, lay the body over them, and use the iron to fuse it to the fabric, thus holding the wings to the jumper.

12 Using the dark brown thread, outline around the bee's body with several rows of straight stitch. Use the same method to embroider several stripes across the body.

13 Position the butterfly wings on the jumper and lay the body over them. Use the iron to fuse the body to the fabric, attaching the wings to the jumper at the same time.

14 Using the dark brown thread, outline the butterfly's body with several rows of straight stitch, ensuring that you stitch over the base of the wings to hold them firmly in place. Use the same method to embroider antennae.

15 Finish off the large flowers with a pink shisha mirror hand-stitched to the center of each.

16 Add extra detail by sewing a couple of ladybug buttons onto the leaves.

17 Work a line of running stitch with three strands of gray embroidery floss to trace the bee's flight path.

18 Embellish the butterflies with a scattering of tiny sequins stitched to the wings and antennae by hand.

Ideas Gallery machine appliqué

Striking appliqué designs can be created using layers of fabric. Choose shapes with simple, bold outlines.

➤ **Sheer fabrics** can be used to create interesting shaded effects. Organza ribbons in different widths and colors are applied to the ground cloth, using a small zigzag stitch. New colors are created where the ribbons overlap.

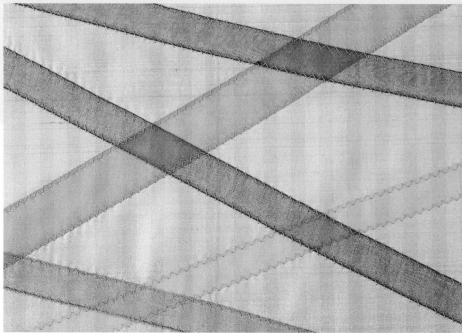

◄ **Playing with scale** can create interesting effects. Squares of a small gingham cloth are applied to a larger gingham fabric using fusible web. The squares are edged with a decorative stitch in contrasting colors and then embellished with purchased flower trims and buttons.

⋀ **Build up motifs** with simple leaf shapes cut from printed fabric and attached to the checkered fabric. Use free-motion machine embroidery to suggest veins and a stem.

◄ **Create motifs** with a dimensional quality by attaching only part of the shape to the background. This simple felt flower is sewn with satin stitch around the center only, leaving the petals free.

▼ **Soften the edges** of appliqué motifs by working over them with free-motion machine embroidery. This velvet heart is adhered to the silk ground with fusible web, then edged and framed with embroidery in variegated and metallic threads.

◄ **Make designs more complex** by layering fabrics. The large heart motif is applied with fusible web and stitched with satin stitch before a smaller heart is added in the same way. Narrow the satin stitch to produce neat corners.

Patchwork and Piecing

Cutting out small pieces of fabric and sewing them back together has been a source of fascination to sewers for many generations. Today patchwork and piecing are more popular than ever, because of their unlimited potential to produce beautifully decorative sewing projects. Enjoy the techniques in the following pages and make them uniquely your own in future sewing projects.

Hand and machine piecing

Patchwork involves sewing small pieces of varied fabric together to create a larger design. You can create pieced designs like the ones shown on pages 68–73 quickly and easily by using rotary cutting equipment and a sewing machine; you may also find that you enjoy the slower pace of hand piecing, especially at times when you just want to curl up in an easy chair and sew.

Fabric preparation

Follow these tips when working with quilting fabrics, as well as napped fabrics.

Quilting Fabrics

Today we have a wider array of beautiful cotton fabrics to choose from than ever before. Look for medium-weight cottons, in a range of values from light to medium, dark, and very dark. To prepare cotton fabrics for piecing, it's a good idea to machine wash them in warm water and dry them with your dryer set to a cotton-appropriate heat level. Press cotton fabrics after they are dry to keep them flat, wrinkle-free, and ready for piecing.

Napped Fabrics

Certain fabrics feature what is called "nap," or a raised, directional surface. If you move your hand gently along a fabric with nap, such as velvet, velveteen, or corduroy, you'll be able to tell in which direction the fabric surface feels smooth. If you slide your hand in the opposite direction, you will feel the roughness of going against the nap. If you are thinking of using a napped fabric for patchwork, the nap can cause the fabric to creep when you join piece together so careful pinning and basting will be required to overcome this.

sewSMART

When using napped fabric, check the manufacturer's laundering directions on the end of the bolt board to make sure that its cleaning method will work for the project you have in mind. For example, if you wish to add patchwork elements to a blouse that can be machine washed and dried, you might decide not to include a napped fabric that can only be dry-cleaned.

Setting up your sewing machine

To set up your sewing machine for maximum efficiency, place it on an uncluttered surface, with plenty of space for laying out the materials. Insert a needle of a suitable size and set the machine for straight stitching, with a medium stitch length. Thread the top of the machine and the bobbin with 100 percent cotton sewing thread.

Test the tension by sewing across two pieces of scrap fabric before you begin a project. For patchwork, you will need to be able to sew accurate ¼ in. (6 mm) seam allowances consistently. Measure the distance from the needle of your machine to the edge of the presser foot. If this distance is precisely ¼ in. (6 mm), you can align the edges of your fabric with the edge of the presser foot as you sew.

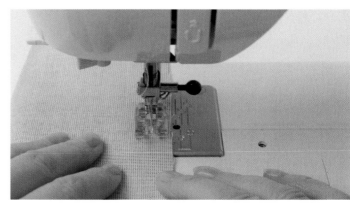

Line up the cut edges of the fabric with the measurement mark you require the seam allowance to be, and sew. Keep the edge of the fabric running along the mark and the seam will be straight.

If this does not produce an accurate seam allowance, however, measure exactly ¼ in. (6 mm) to the right of the needle, and place a piece of low-tack masking tape on the throat plate at that distance. The tape will serve as the guide for the fabric edges as you sew.

Using a rotary cutter and quilter's ruler

Quilter's rulers are marked in increments that are easy to see when placed over fabric. A rotary cutter has a razor-sharp round blade that cuts accurate shapes very quickly. A self-healing cutting mat will allow the rotary cutter blade to cut easily and precisely while protecting your work surface.

A 6 in. (15 cm) square is being cut from a 6 in. (15 cm)-wide fabric strip. The left hand is positioned away from the right edge of the ruler, holding the ruler on the fabric. The right hand slides the rotary cutter blade along the right edge of the ruler as it cuts. Be sure to close the blade guard after each cut to avoid injuring yourself.

Half- and quarter-square triangles

Half-square triangles can be made by cutting a square diagonally. Cutting the resulting triangles in half makes four quarter-square triangles. The triangles are often used in combination with other shapes to create some of the more complex patterns that are featured in many traditional patchwork designs.

1 To make a half-square triangle, cut a square of fabric in the size required for your project. Lay the square on a cutting mat and cut along the diagonal with a rotary cutter.

2 To make a quarter triangle, lay the ruler over a half-square triangle, positioning it so that the straight edge runs from the point to the base. Cut along the edge of the ruler.

3 To join either half- or quarter-square triangles, stitch them together taking a ¼ in. (6 mm) seam allowance. Press the seams allowances toward the darker fabric as you join each piece.

4 Four half-square triangles are joined to make two squares.

sewSMART

Check your local fabric store or quilt shop and compare different types of rotary cutters before you purchase one. Some have to be opened manually while others have a blade that retracts when you push on the cutter. Find the features you like best and the cutter you find easiest to use.

Machine piecing

With today's fast cutting and machine piecing techniques and a sewing machine, you can create beautiful patchwork designs easily. The strip piecing techniques below are ideal for creating patchwork fabric for projects of all sizes.

1 Cut a 3 x 45 in. (7.5 x 114 cm) strip from three different fabrics. Sew the three strips together lengthwise, using a ¼ in. (6 mm) seam allowance to produce vertically striped fabric. Press.

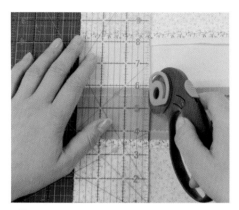

2 Rotary cut across the vertically striped fabric to make a 3 in. (7.5 cm)-wide segment. Repeat, for a total of three segments.

3 Sew the segments together, offsetting the squares on each strip by one. Match and pin the seams, then sew. Press the seams open.

Hand piecing

Hand piecing is a popular technique. Although it is slower than piecing by machine, it offers a greater opportunity for accuracy in difficult piecing tasks, such as making multiple points meet perfectly at the center of a star. Try the following techniques and see if you like the results they give you.

Using purchased templates

Metal and plastic templates are readily available in a variety of shapes and sizes, and can be used repeatedly. Commercial hand piecing templates do not include a ¼ in. (6 mm) seam allowance. Follow these steps to use this type of template.

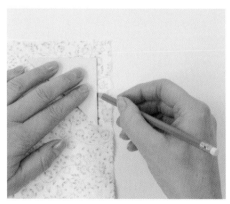

1 Place the template on the right side of your chosen fabric. Holding it securely in place, use a fabric-marking pencil to mark around each edge of the template.

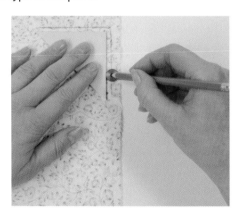

2 Using either an acrylic quilter's ruler or a ¼ in. (6 mm)-round quilter's disk (see page 11), carefully mark a ¼ in. (6 mm) seam allowance around edge of template. Cut along the marked outside lines.

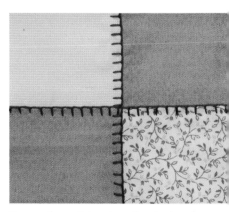

To sew the patches together by hand, begin and end ¼ in. (6 mm) in from the ends of the patches. Take running stitches through layers, beginning and ending with a knot. Press seam allowances to one side.

Basting over interfacing

To use nonwoven, fusible interfacing for cutting and sewing very precise patchwork designs by hand, follow these simple steps.

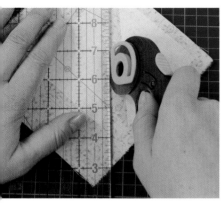

1 Trace the finished size of the shapes onto the dull (or matte-finish) side of nonwoven fusible interfacing, omitting all seam allowances. Cut the shapes out, and carefully press them onto the wrong side of an appropriate fabric, following manufacturer's directions and leaving at least ½ in. (12 mm) between each shape. Cut out each patch, adding an accurate ¼ in. (6 mm) seam allowance to each edge.

2 Fold the seam allowances over each edge of the fused shape and thread-baste them in place, making sure to fold the corners neatly.

Embellishments

Once your patchwork is assembled, enhance it with decorative details.

Topstitch patches using topstitching thread. Stitch around the edge of patches ¼ in. (6 mm) from the seams, pivoting carefully at corners to ensure accuracy.

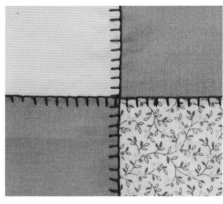

Embroidery stitches can be used as patchwork embellishments. Here, patches are edged with blanket stitch (see page 16).

Oversewing

This quick hand-piecing method produces a very strong seam. Follow these steps to oversew patches together by hand.

Slip Stitch (or Ladder Stitch)

This technique produces a flat, invisible join between patches. A weaker join than an oversewn seam, it should be used only on patchwork backed by another fabric.

Place two interfaced and basted patches right sides together. Thread a needle and knot thread end. Bring thread from back through the fold at the right end of patches. Insert the needle tip ⅛ in. (3 mm) beyond the exit point of thread, working from back of patch toward you. Continue, taking tiny stitches to the end.

Place two interfaced patches together, wrong sides facing. Thread a needle and knot end. Pass needle through both patches. Insert needle into the fold of the patch in back, opposite the exit point of thread. Move the needle ⅛ in. (2 mm) inside the fold of the back patch and bring it out. Insert the needle in the fold of the patch nearest you. Continue stitching to end.

Tiny beads can add detail to patchwork. These beads are sewn on using the backstitch method (see page 17), with just one bead on the needle at a time.

Patchwork throw

In this colorful strip-pieced patchwork throw, some of the strips were decorated with machine embroidery to add extra interest, and the blanket has been backed with cozy fleece for extra warmth. You can easily use any remaining patchwork to make a matching pillow.

Materials

- 20 x 45 in. (50 x 114 cm) of eight different fabrics, including six different blue-and-white striped fabrics; one red, blue, and white striped fabric; and one red-and-white check fabric
- Red and white sewing thread
- 16 x 44 in. (40 x 112 cm) of red cotton fabric
- 245 in. (422 cm) of medium piping cord
- 60 x 60 in. (152 x 152 cm) of cream fleece fabric
- Embroidery needle
- Red embroidery floss
- Tape measure
- Ruler
- Rotary cutter and cutting mat
- Scissors
- Sewing machine

Techniques

- Using decorative stitches, page 67
- Fabric preparation, page 64
- Setting up your sewing machine, page 64
- Machine piecing, page 66
- Making piping, page 93

The finished throw will measure approximately 59 x 59 in. (150 x 150 cm).

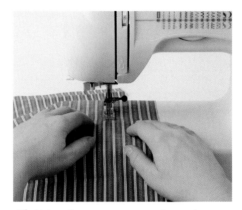

1 Using the rotary cutter, ruler and cutting mat, cut one 9 in. (23 cm) strip lengthwise from each of the eight pieces of fabric. Using the red sewing thread and a decorative machine stitch, embroider a line 2¾ in. (7 cm) from one edge of one of the blue-and-white striped pieces.

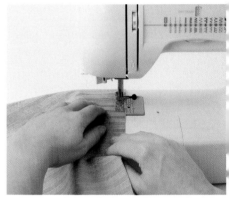

2 Right-sides together, join all eight strips along the long edges with white thread and a ¼ in. (6 mm) seam allowance. Repeat steps 1 and 2 with eight more 9 in. (23 cm) strips of fabric, but embroider two lines on the same blue-and-white fabric, and join the strips in a different arrangement.

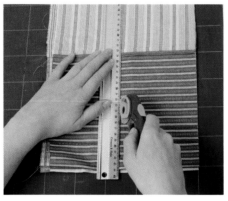

3 Carefully fold the pieces of fabric into four, aligning seams and raw edges. Using the rotary cutter on the cutting mat, cut the pieces into 5 in. (12.5 cm)-wide strips. You will be able to cut 18 strips—you need 13 for the throw and the rest can be used to make a matching pillow.

4 Join the strips together in a brick pattern. Fold each rectangle in half lengthways and pinch the edge to make a crease. Align these creases with the seams on another strip and pin together. Sew the strips together with a ¼ in. (6 mm) seam allowance. The finished piece of patchwork needs to be 13 strips of 8 rectangles each.

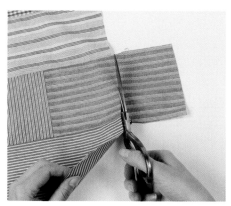

5 At the ends of the patchwork, half of some of the rectangles will protrude. Carefully cut these off to create a straight edge, as shown. Round off the corners of the patchwork throw with the scissors.

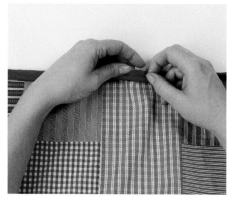

6 Make piping using the red fabric and piping cord. Starting away from the corner, pin the piping around all four sides of the throw, aligning the raw edges. Machine stitch in place, starting 4 in. (10 cm) from the raw end of the piping.

7 Near the end of the piping, stop 2½ in. (6 cm) from where you started. Do not cut off excess piping. Remove stitching next to the cord between starting and stopping points. Move the cord aside, join ends of the fabric. Trim seam allowance to ¼ in. (6 mm).

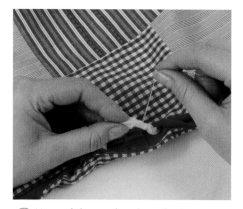

8 Unravel the cord ends and cut away half its bulk. Twist the thinned ends together over ¾ in. (2 cm), ensuring that the new cord fits into piping fabric. Trim excess cord. Bind the twisted section with thread to hold it together. Sew the gap in the piping closed; finish stitching it onto throw.

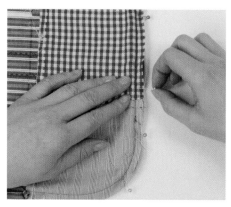

9 Lay the fleece on a flat surface. Right sides together, lay the patchwork on top and trim to match. Align raw edges and ensure that there are no creases. Pin then machine stitch the two layers together, with a ¼ in. (6 mm) seam allowance and leaving a 6¾ in. (17 cm) opening in one side.

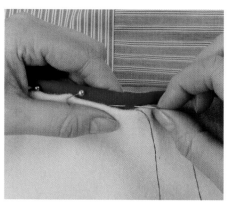

10 Turn the throw right side out through the opening, and push out the corners and seams carefully. Close the opening with slip stitches.

11 Using the red floss, tie separate knots over some of the joins in the patchwork in a symmetrical pattern.

sewSMART

You can create four different 5 in. (13 cm)-wide strips by turning half of each of the two batches upside down, thus rearranging the order in which the fabrics run. When joining the strips together to make the patchwork, every fifth strip will be a repeat of a previous one, which gives an interesting random effect.

Lavender pillow

Traditional techniques combined with modern materials make this delicate pillow a lovely addition to any room. Small scraps of silk in similar shades are sewn together to create the pillow. It can be made as a keepsake, using scraps of fabric from a wedding or christening gown, or newly designed for a ring pillow in a marriage ceremony.

Materials

- Selection of cream-patterned, cream, and gray silk fabrics
- Iron-on interfacing
- Cream sewing thread
- Dark cream and gray embroidery floss
- White basting thread
- 8¾ in. (22 cm)-square of pearl gray silk fabric
- Cotton or polyester batting
- 36 in. (91 cm) of decorative lace trim
- Quilter's ruler
- Rotary cutter and cutting mat
- Scissors
- Iron
- Dried lavender
- Embroidery needle
- Two 4¾ in. (12 cm)-square pieces of cream silk organza fabric
- Pinking shears

Techniques

- Feathered chain stitch, page 19
- Using a rotary cutter and quilter's rule, page 65
- Basting over interfacing, page 67
- Oversewing, page 67
- Attaching trim, page 90

1 Using the quilter's ruler, rotary cutter, and mat, cut nine 2¾ in. (7 cm) squares of interfacing. Cut each square in half diagonally to make 18 triangles. Iron each triangle onto a piece of silk fabric and cut around it, leaving a ¼ in. (6 mm) seam allowance. Turn the edges of the silk over the interfacing; baste in place.

2 Using the oversewing technique, sew two triangles together along the long edge to make a square.

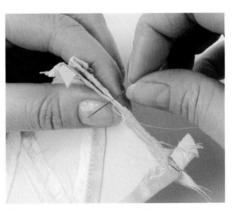

3 Oversew three squares together to make a strip. Repeat this twice more, then sew all three strips together to make a large square. Pull out the basting threads and press the square, pressing the seam allowances around the edges open.

4 Embroider lines of feathered chain stitch (see page 19) to define the edges of the nine squares. Embroider the two lines in one direction with cream floss and the two in the other direction with gray floss.

5 With right sides together and aligning raw edges, pin the square of pearl gray silk to the patchwork. Leaving a 2 in. (5 cm) opening in one side, machine stitch around the four edges, taking a ¼ in. (6 mm) seam allowance all around.

6 Turn the pillow right side out through the opening.

7 Stuff the batting through the opening in the side of the patterned cushion. Work batting into each of the corners to make them full and square; and loosely stuff the central part.

8 Leaving a small opening in one edge, machine stitch the two squares of silk organza together, taking a ½ in. (12 mm) seam allowance. Pink the edges of the fabric. Fill the sachet with dried lavender through the opening then hand stitch the opening closed.

9 Slip the lavender sachet into the cushion so that it sits on top of the batting, underneath the patchwork. Push in a little more batting under the sachet to fill out the cushion, but be careful not make it too firm.

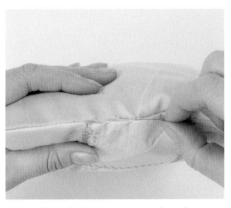

sewSMART

If you would like to use your own selection of fabrics, be sure to choose light fabrics that are of similar weights. Silk and fine lightweight cotton will work the best.

10 Slip stitch the opening closed.

11 Slip stitch the trimming around the edges of the pillow.

Combining fabrics

Both commercial and vintage laces can be used to add beautiful accents to a patchwork or sewing project. You can work with lace fabric, panels of lace, or individual lace motifs. With new lace, check the printed information on the bolt for the manufacturer's laundering instructions to make sure it will be compatible with the other fabrics in your project. If you're using vintage lace, make sure it can be laundered alongside the other fabrics you are using.

Individual lace motifs
Adding an isolated or single lace motif is easy with the following technique.

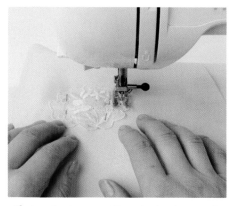

1 Lay the lace motif on the background fabric. Lay these on top of a piece of tear-away stabilizer. Pin the three layers together. Sew around the edge of the lace shape, using a small zigzag stitch.

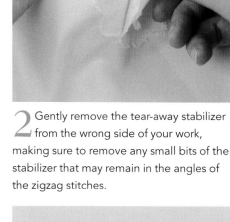

2 Gently remove the tear-away stabilizer from the wrong side of your work, making sure to remove any small bits of the stabilizer that may remain in the angles of the zigzag stitches.

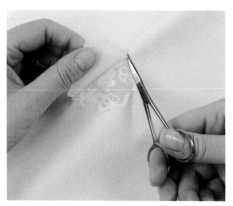

3 Use a pair of small, sharp-tipped scissors to cut the background fabric from underneath the lace motif, taking care not to snip into the lace.

4 Place a clean, white cloth on an ironing board, and position the finished lace motif on top of it. The lace and the stitching around it should lie smooth and flat. Place a cloth on top of the lace and press with an iron.

Lace inserts

This is a neat way of inserting a strip of narrow lace between two pieces of fabric.

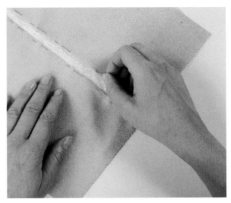

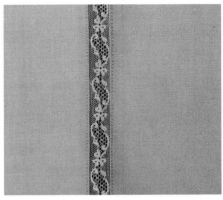

1 Using pinking shears, pink the two fabrics that will go either side of the lace panel. Turn under and press a ¼ in. (6 mm) seam allowance along all these edges.

2 Position the pressed edge of a fabric ⅛ in. (3 mm) over the long edge of the lace, and pin the two pieces together. Repeat with pressed edge of second fabric, on the other long edge of the lace panel.

3 Using a straight stitch, topstitch one edge of the fabric to the lace panel ¹⁄₁₆ in. (1 mm) in from the edge of fabric, catching the long edge of lace panel as you go. Repeat on the other long edge; press.

Lace fabric

The delicate threads and slightly raised textures of many of today's lace fabrics can sometimes be tricky to use. Backing lace fabric with another fabric will stabilize it and make it easier to handle.

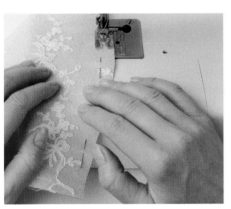

Vintage fabrics

Consider the quality of any vintage fabric you use. Be aware that such fabrics can sometimes become unstable, with weakened fibers. Avoid fabrics like these in favor of newer, more durable ones.

If you choose to work with vintage lace, it's a good idea to make sure that it can be laundered in the same way as the other fabrics you wish to use. Try washing a small scrap of the vintage lace by hand using a gentle soap and allow it to air dry; then check to see if shrinkage, distortions, or discolorations have occurred. If the lace looks unacceptable, you may wish to discard it and substitute another in your project.

Stabilizing fabrics

Thin, loosely woven, or unstable fabrics can benefit from extra support before being incorporated into pieced projects. You can layer them over a firm fabric or fuse a layer of iron-on interfacing to the wrong side; choose the technique that best suits your fabric. Use iron-on interfacing to balance the thickness of a thin fabric.

Layering fabrics

If you cannot find prewashed muslin, wash plain muslin and iron it before use.

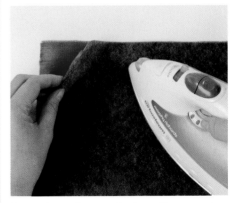

Cut a piece of prewashed muslin or sew-in interfacing to fabric size. Pin, then baste the layers together around the edges.

Ironing on interfacing

Choose a fusible interfacing in the appropriate weight for the main fabric in your project. Cut the interfacing slightly smaller than the fabric to avoid getting adhesive on your ironing board. Place the interfacing with the bubbled (shiny side) up. Place the fabric right side up on top and press the two together. Follow the manufacturer's instructions, and do not slide the iron over the fabric; instead, lift it up and place it down again on each new area.

Seam techniques

For patchwork, a simple straight seam with a ¼ in. (6 mm) seam allowance is used most often. This is a narrower seam allowance than ones called for in many other types of sewing projects. Here are four of the most useful types of seams.

French seam

This technique finishes two edges of fabric at the same time and it is particularly good for sheer fabrics or seams with a shallow curve.

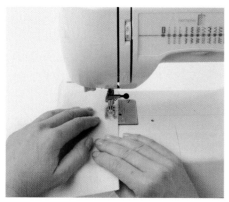

1 Place the two fabrics to be joined with the wrong sides together. Using a ¼ in. (6mm) seam allowance, stitch them together with a simple straight stitch.

2 Trim the seam allowance to a scant ⅛ in. (3 mm), as shown, and press to one side. Refold the two fabrics along the seam line with right sides together.

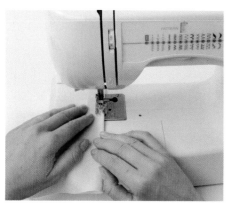

3 Stitch ¼ in. (6 mm) from the folded edge to encase the raw edges of the trimmed seam allowance.

4 On the right side, the seam looks like a straight seam. The wrong side has a narrow pocket that covers the raw edges.

sew**SMART**

Another way of creatively piecing sections of delicate lace or batiste fabrics together is to join them using strips of entredeux—which is a band of fabric with hemstitched holes down the middle and fabric borders the size of seam widths. You can either seam each lace or fabric piece up to the hemstitching line or overlap each piece over the entredeux and stitch with a narrow zigzag stitch.

Flat-fell seam

This technique is suitable for straight seams on light- and medium-weight fabrics. It encloses the edges and joins the fabrics together.

Pinked seams

Use pinking shears to finish the edges and keep them from fraying.

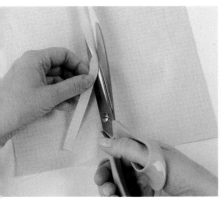

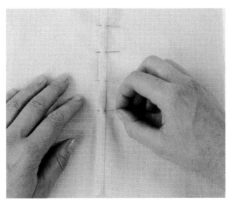

1 Place the fabrics together with wrong sides facing and with a ⅝ in. (1.5 cm) seam allowance, sew them together with straight stitch. Press the seam allowance to one side, trim the underseam allowance to ⅛ in. (3mm).

2 Press under ¼ in. (6mm) of the outer seam allowance. Pin the seam allowance flat to the fabric.

1 To start, place two fabrics together with the right sides facing. Straight-stitch them together, using a ⅝ in. (1.5 cm) seam allowance. Using pinking shears, trim the raw edges of the seam allowances to ½ in. (12 mm).

3 Using a straight seam, sew close to the pressed fold.

4 The finished flat-fell seam is strong and has a neat appearance on both sides.

2 This will minimize bulk in the seam allowance area and help prevent the seam allowance from showing through on the right side of the fabric after the seam is pressed.

Topstitched seams

This method can be used on both straight and curved seams, and is suitable for light-, medium-, and even heavyweight fabrics.

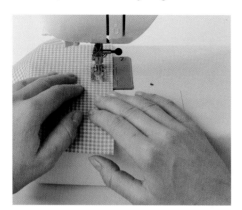

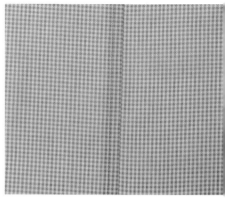

1 Place the two fabrics to be joined right sides together. Using a straight machine stitch, sew them together, taking a ⅝ in. (1.5 cm) seam allowance. Overlock or pink the raw edges and press the seam allowance to one side.

2 Working on the right side of the fabric, topstitch through both the fabric and the underlying seam allowance, working ⅓ in. (1 cm) from the seam.

3 Just one line of topstitching has been used, but you can do more than one line for a decorative effect if you like. You can also use a twin needle to produce two consistent lines of stitching.

sewSMART

The top stitch seam is designed to be both decorative and functional. To ensure a straight stitch with this seam and others, sight the fabric and not the needle while sewing.

Pieced skirt

Piecing can be used to personalize garments by combining fabrics and features from other pieces of clothing. In this project, the fabrics and details from two garments have been incorporated into a new skirt. It was easy to simply remove panels from one skirt and replace them with pieced and patched fabric from other garments. It is also possible to piece fabrics directly onto the ground fabric.

Materials

- Skirt with flat-fell seamed panels
- Thin paper to make pattern
- Various pieces from other garments, including pockets, belt loops, pieces with seams
- Sewing threads to match fabrics
- Dressmaker's scissors
- Pencil
- Air-erasable fabric marker
- Pins
- Pinking shears
- Scissors
- Sewing machine

Techniques

- Combining fabrics, page 74
- Pinked seams, page 77
- Topstitched seam, page 78

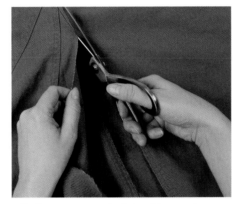

1 Cut out a panel of the skirt, cutting carefully, as close as possible to the flat-fell seams.

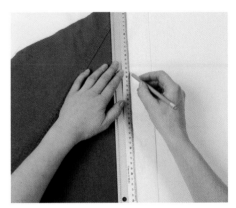

2 Lay the cut panel on the thin pattern paper and draw around it to make a paper pattern.

3 Arrange a selection of other garment pieces on a flat work surface. Use existing flat-fell seams or fold under any raw edges and butt the pieces together where you want them.

4 Lay the pattern piece carefully over the arrangement of fabric pieces. Make sure that all the areas you want to use are contained within it.

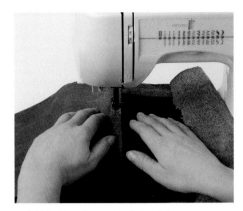

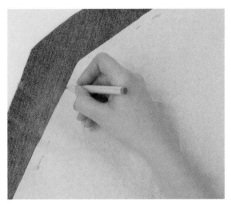

5 Pin all of the pieces together, through all of the layers. Iron the pinned pieces to press any folded edges. Carefully take out the pins and, using pinking shears, trim any excess fabric behind the pieces to a seam allowance of ½ in. (1 cm). Reassemble and pin the pieces in the required arrangement.

6 Working from the right side, sew the pieces together, matching your stitching to any original topstitching, adjusting the stitch length, shade, and weight of thread accordingly. Using one seaming technique and color thread throughout can help to unify the various fabrics and elements.

7 Lay the pattern over the joined fabrics and draw around it with an air-erasable fabric marker. Add a seam allowance of ½ in. (1 cm) to any edges that will be sewn into the skirt.

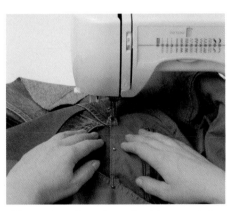

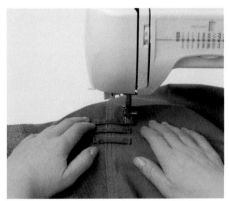

8 Pin the pieced panel behind the opening in the skirt, matching the drawn line with the edges of the skirt where the panel was originally cut out.

9 Working from the right side, topstitch the new panel in place, re-hemming the pieced panel and the skirt, if necessary.

10 Finish by machine stitching on any desired decorative details, such as belt loops.

sewSMART

If your skirt has plain seams rather than flat-fell seams, rip out the panel stitching rather than cutting the panel out as shown in Step 1.

Window treatment

Incorporating lace lets daylight filter through this window treatment. The light illuminates the delicate design. Start by cutting a flat panel of fabric to the size appropriate for your window, and arrange the pieces of lace around the edges and within it, placing each as desired.

Materials

- Ivory organza cut to the width of the finished window panel and long enough to provide for a rod pocket at the top
- Selection of lace pieces that can be arranged in a design to suit your window; this example uses a strip of edging lace, a lace collar, and a lace motif
- Lace pins
- Ivory sewing thread
- Curtain rod
- Tape measure
- Sharp scissors
- Sewing machine

Techniques

- Individual lace motifs, page 74
- Using tear-away stabilizer, page 51

sewSMART

When applying lace to fabrics that are less stable than silk organza, it may be necessary to use tear-away stabilizer (see page 51).

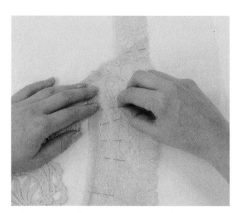

1 Arrange the lace pieces on the organza, with the lace strip as the leading edge. Pin in place, aligning the outer edge of the lace strip with the edge of the organza.

2 Use a narrow zigzag stitch to sew the inner edges of the lace pieces to the organza. Follow a line in the lace so when you cut away the excess, the edge is neat. As you move from one piece of lace to another, choose a stitching path that blends with each lace pattern.

3 Use sharp-tipped scissors and carefully cut away any lace remaining beyond the line of stitching. Turn the curtain panel over and cut away the excess organza behind the lace pieces.

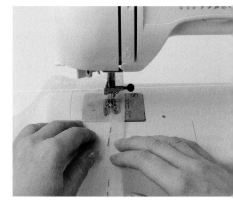

4 Finish opposite edge with a double seam. Establish the finished length of the window panel (trim the top of the panel if necessary). Turn under a narrow hem, then turn under a casing wide enough to hold your curtain rod. Machine stitch along the bottom edge of the casing.

Ideas Gallery patchwork and piecing

These patchwork patterns are in many different color schemes and styles. Study those that appeal to you immediately and think how to use them in your sewing projects.

➤ **Using seams** to add texture. This Formal Garden block is pieced with half- and quarter-square triangles. The active print fabric draws the eye toward the center of the design.

▼ **Decorative border.** Two fabrics are featured in the Double Sawtooth border, with a third fabric in the center of the design, which could be decorated with embroidery or appliqué.

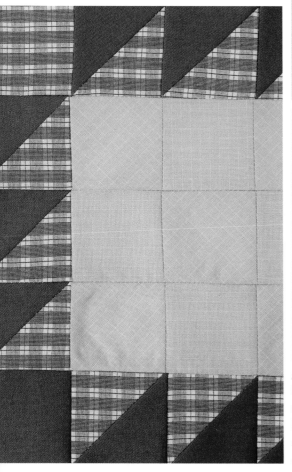

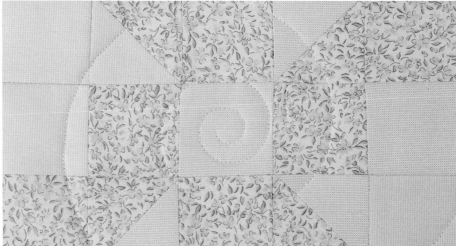

⋀ **Overlaying patterns** adds texture and interest. A "propeller" design in two different fabrics has subtle texture added by quilting the block to a layer of batting and topstitching a spiral motif that radiates out from the central square.

➤ Adding beads highlights elements of the design with a touch of sparkle. This Card Basket block features beads that are couched along the seams of certain shapes.

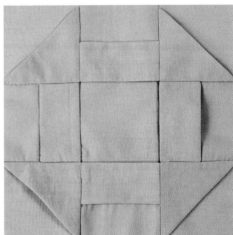

⋀ Applying a relief design made as a separate piece. The relief element is applied to the background block of nine squares by slipstitching it partway along the short edges of the triangles. To form the rectangles, fold a square in half, right sides facing and sew along three edges. Turn fabric through, press, and slipstitch opening closed. Repeat method to create triangle, but folding on the diagonal. Slipstitch components together as shown.

◄ Adding dimensional sections to create visual interest. This design, based on the "z and cross" formation has contrasting "fins" added diagonally across some squares. To make each fin cut a square of contrasting fabric the same size as the background squares and fold it in half diagonally, right sides together. Sew around the two open edges, leaving a small opening. Clip and turn the triangle through. Slipstitch the opening closed. Slip stitch the fins diagonally across the selected squares.

➤ **Strip-pieced rectangles** are an effective way of combining fabrics. This four-color patchwork pattern is very easy to make, using the machine piecing techniques on page 66.

▼ **A strip-pieced brick design** is created by setting rectangles so that each block is centered on the seam of the adjacent row. In this example, four different fabrics create an interwoven look.

⋏ **Adding topstitching** to highlight seams. This Weathervane panel consists of one dark and two lighter fabrics. Machine stitching a narrow zigzag in a contrast color makes a feature of some of the seams in the design.

◄ **Using stripes** to create a steplike effect. This traditional design, known as London Steps, features two fabrics rotated.

⋏ **Lines of topstitching** replace the need to work with many different fabrics and add a touch of dimension to this pattern.

◄ **Hand-embroidered crazy patchwork** is a traditional way of using small scraps of fabric. The edges of each piece are turned under, as for hand appliqué, and stitched to a background fabric. Feather stitch embroidery covers the seams and adds sheen.

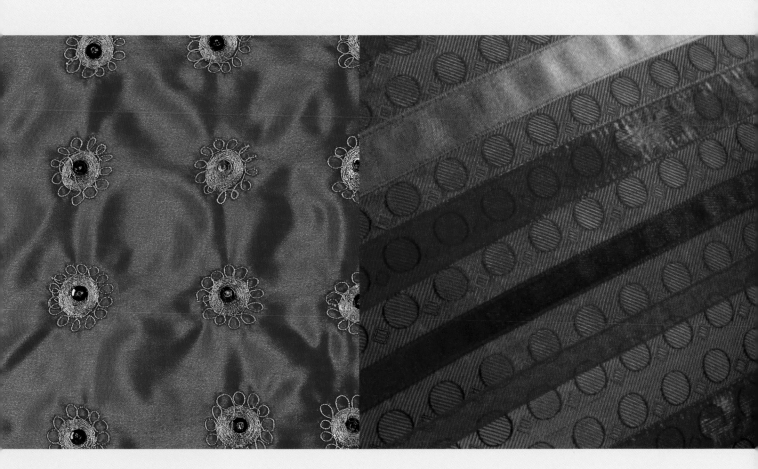

Embellishments and Beading

One of the easiest ways to personalize an item is simply to sew on a decoration. Between the vast range of commercially available embellishments and the opportunity of creating your own, the possibilities for decorating existing or self-made items are almost infinite.

Embellishments

Embellishments can be used to revitalize a tired item, add detail or glamour to a plain one, or update a favorite. Adding embellishments is something that should be considered at the outset of any project, because careful selection and application of materials and trims can transform any design into something uniquely special.

Choosing and attaching trims

Trims are available by the yard (meter) at most fabric and craft stores. Although they are usually applied to a project in strips, sometimes trims can be cut up into smaller sections, so that individual motifs can be stitched onto a project. This can be a great way to make a very small amount of trim go quite a long way. If necessary, be sure that the trim you select is fully washable, and that it is not too heavy for the fabric you will be using for your project.

Techniques used to attach trims will vary, depending both on the type of trim and the nature of the base fabric. Sometimes you simply apply trims with a line of machine stitching; however, there are some instances when hand sewing may be required. Occasionally it can be acceptable to resort to using fabric glue to attach trims, especially on items such as lamp shades that are not washed and will only be lightly handled.

Ribbons

Ribbons are very versatile, with a multitude of applications for all types of sewing project. As well as being available in a huge variety of widths, colors, and designs, ribbons have the advantage of having finished, non-fraying edges.

You can apply ribbons flat or gathered directly onto the fabric surface, or make them into separate decorations that can be stitched in place after the rest of the project has been sewn.

Gathered ribbons
You can make elegant ruffles quickly and easily from ribbon.

1 Set your sewing machine to a long straight stitch and, using matching sewing thread, sew down the center of the ribbon. Secure the threads at one end and pull one thread at the other end to gather up the ribbon to the required length.

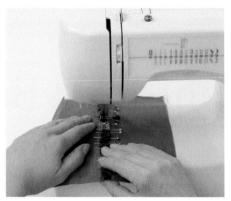

2 Pin the gathered ribbon to the fabric with plenty of pins set at right angles to the ribbon, to hold it securely in place. Set your sewing machine to a medium straight stitch and stitch the gathered ribbon to the fabric down the center. Carefully pull out the gathering threads.

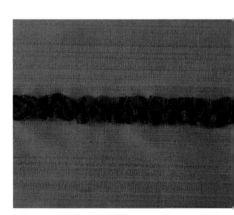

3 The resulting ruffles can be dense, as shown above, or soft, depending on the quantity of ribbon used.

Threads and yarns

Threads and yarns might seem unpromising as decorative materials, but they can be made into classic embellishments. Twisted into cords, formed into tassels, or used for couching, threads and yarns can offer unique color combinations.

Making cord

Cords are easier to make with the help of a friend, who can hold one end while you twist the other.

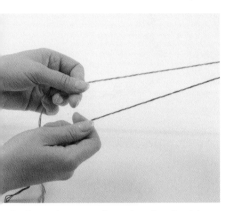

1 Cut at least two lengths of embroidery floss, each 30 percent longer than size of finished cord. Knot them together at one end. Divide the strands evenly into two groups. Ask a friend to hold the knotted end, or tie it to something steady. Holding one group of strands in each hand, twist them in the same direction.

2 Continue twisting until the twisted floss starts to kink up. Hold both ends together firmly in one hand and ask your friend to let go of the knotted end. Allow the twisted strands to coil up and twist around one another. When they have all stopped moving, pull the cord out straight and knot the free ends together.

3 A great advantage of making your own cord is that you can choose floss colors to complement your project perfectly.

Making a tassel

Tassels are another easy-to-make embellishment that will find a home on many projects.

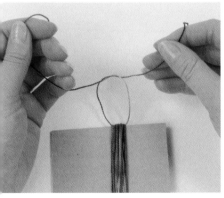

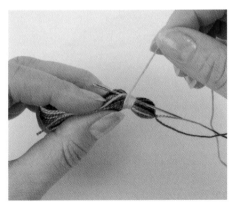

1 Cut a piece of cardboard in the length you want the finished tassel to be; this one is 2⅜ in. (6 cm). Wind embroidery floss around it 20–30 times, depending on how full you want the tassel skirt to be. Slide a length of floss, or a twisted cord, under the wound loops and tie it in a firm double knot at the top edge of the cardboard, as shown. Slide the loops off.

2 Wrap a length of floss around the tassel ⅝ in. (15 mm) from the top. Lay a tapestry needle over the wrap, with the eye toward the skirt of the tassel, as shown. Wrap the floss neatly and smoothly around the tassel and needle a few more times. Thread the needle with the end of the floss and pull it through the wrap to secure it. Trim the end close to the wrap.

3 Cut through the lower loops of the tassel, trimming the ends even, if necessary. As with cord, the range of floss colors available allows you to make a tassel to match almost any project. This one is made from variegated embroidery floss, with the neck bound in a single color.

Bias binding

Bias binding is made from a strip of fabric cut at an angle of 45 degrees from the selvedge. Cut at this angle, the fabric has most stretch and give, so it can be used to finish straight or curved raw edges by encasing them. It can also provide a contrasting decorative trim. Bias binding is often used to provide a neat finish on sheer or lightweight fabrics, where conventional hems would show through. Commercial bias binding are available, but you can make your own, using the various sizes of bias binding makers sold in good sewing stores. Generally, thicker fabrics need wider binding, while narrower binding is suitable for medium- and lightweight cottons.

Making continuous bias tape

Continuous bias strips can be used to make bias binding or to cover piping cord. You will need a purchased bias binding maker, available in sewing stores.

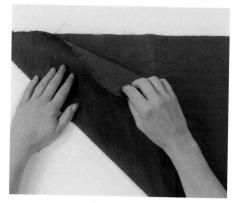

1 Cut a strip of the full fabric width by 16 in. (40 cm). Fold one end over to form a triangle. Press the fold, then cut along the pressed line.

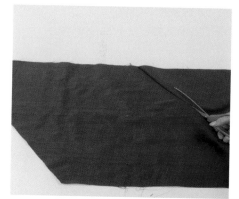

2 Fold the other end of fabric to form a triangle, ensuring that the slanted line slopes in the same direction as the line cut in Step 1. Cut along the pressed fold.

3 Cut a strip of cardboard as advised on the tape maker pack. Start at one of the slanted ends of the fabric and use the strip to draw parallel lines across the fabric.

4 With right sides facing, pin the straight edges of fabric together, matching the drawn lines at the seam line, so one width of binding extends beyond the edges on either side. Check the join by opening out the fabric either side of the pinned seam.

5 Stitch along the pinned line then press the seam allowance open. Starting at one end, cut along the drawn lines until the tube of fabric has become one long strip of bias-cut tape.

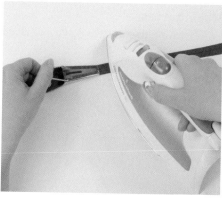

6 To turn the tape into bias binding, feed one end of the strip into the tape maker. Pull the tape maker along the strip, ironing the bias tape as it comes out. The bias tape is now ready to use.

Purchased motifs

In addition to trims, many sew-on or iron-on motifs and patches are available. These are a fantastic and very fast way to embellish a project. They often have a whimsical charm well suited for customizing jeans and casual wear, and some (such as iron-on gems) can add a sophisticated touch to a project. Also, letter patches are great for monogrammed projects.

Found objects

Many types of found objects make interesting embellishments. The challenge is to find the best way to attach them to a project, and usually some experimentation is required. If the item has a hole, it can usually be stitched on. Some items, such as shells, can be drilled to make a hole, while others, such as pressed flowers can be placed inside pockets of translucent fabric.

Piping

Piping can be used to add a crisp, decorative edge, define a seam, or make a clear division between different panels of soft furnishing or garment projects. Although it can be purchased in a variety of styles, colors, and widths, it is surprisingly easy to make your own using cord covered in continuous bias strips.

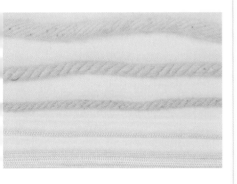

Piping cord

Piping cord can be made from cotton or man-made fibers and is available in a variety of thicknesses, from very fine to almost ropelike weights. If you are using fine or lightweight fabrics, the standard twisted-cord construction can show through the piping, so choose a smoother cord. For very fine piping, roman blind cord can be used. Try to use cord that has the same care requirements as the main fabric. You can prewash cotton cord to avoid shrinkage. The covering for the cord is made from a continuous bias strip, using either the main fabric or a contrasting one. For cord that is up to ¼ in. (6 mm) thick, the bias strip needs to be 1⅜ in. (3.5 cm) wide. For thicker cord, measure the circumference of the cord and add 1 in. (2.5 cm) for seam allowances.

Making and using piping

Follow these steps to make piping for adding definition to a seam in a decorating project.

1 Make a strip of bias tape, following Steps 1–5 of Making continuous bias tape (see page 92). Open the tape out flat and lay a length of piping cord down the middle on the wrong side; then fold the tape in half over it. Insert a zipper foot into your sewing machine and stitch the edges of the tape together, sewing as close to the cord as possible.

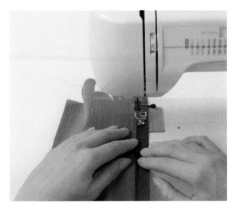

2 Lay the piping on the right side of the fabric, aligning the raw edges. Stitch along the line of stitching that holds the bias tape around the cord.

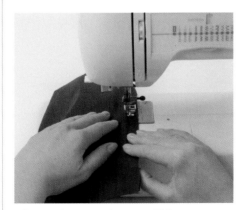

3 Lay the second piece of fabric over the piped piece, aligning the raw edges. Machine stitch through all layers, taking the same seam allowance as in the previous step.

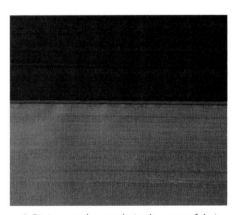

4 Piping can be made in the same fabric as the project for a subtle finish, or in a strong contrast color, as shown above, for a bold look.

Trimmed jacket

Give a purchased jacket designer treatment using this straightforward technique. The decorative bias-cut tape combines with the style of the jacket to produce a rather quirky interpretation of a braided military dress uniform. Lightweight cotton fabric recycled from the back of an old shirt was used to make the bias tape.

Materials

- 14 x 22 in. (35 x 56 cm) piece of fabric for bias strip
- Air-erasable fabric marker
- Sewing thread to match bias fabric
- Pinking shears
- Embroidery needle
- Embroidery floss in color to complement bias fabric

Techniques

- Chain stitch, page 16
- Making continuous bias tape, page 92

1 Cut, mark, and sew the fabric to make a tube from which to cut the bias strip. Mark the lines ½ in. (1cm) apart. Trim the raw edges of the seam allowance with pinking shears to prevent them from fraying. Cut the bias strip.

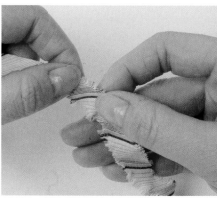

2 Scrape your fingernails over the edges of the cut bias strip, against the grain of the fabric, to ruffle and fray them a little.

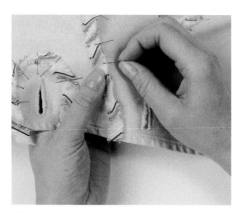

3 Pin the bias strip to the jacket, curving it to make patterns across the front, back, and arms. The patterns can be as elaborate as you wish, just use plenty of pins to hold the bias strip in place.

4 To make the patterns continuous when jacket is opened, mark them on the button band side with an air-erasable marker, then button the jacket up. Repeat the same pattern on the opening side. Repeat this technique where the pattern crosses pocket flaps.

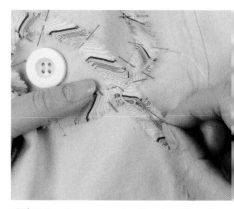

5 Using three strands of embroidery floss and chain stitch, sew along the middle of the bias strip to attach it to the jacket by hand. When the stitching is complete, trim any long ends of the bias tape. Where the cut ends meet the jacket edge, trim them off, leaving them slightly long.

Flower hat

The pretty flowers that adorn this knitted hat could be used to decorate a host of different projects. Make up the different types of flowers first; then arrange them on the project, pinning them in place to create a garland effect. Stitch them on with a bead in the center of each one. Use a few extra flowers to decorate a pair of matching gloves.

Materials

- ⅛ in. (3 mm)-wide ribbon
- Hand-sewing needle
- Sewing thread to match ribbon
- Wide rickrack
- Sewing thread to match rickrack
- Non-fraying fabric, such as Ultrasuede® or felt
- Craft paddle-punch kit in a flower shape
- Cutting mat
- Large and small painted wood beads

Techniques

- Ribbons, page 90
- Choosing and attaching trims, page 90

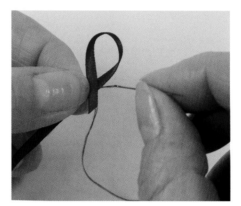

1 To make a ribbon flower, thread the needle, double the thread, and knot both ends. Make a ribbon loop and, from the back, bring the needle through the ends of the loop to join them.

2 Make a second loop, opposite the first one, and take the needle through the free end of it to hold it in place.

3 Continue making loops and taking the thread through them until you have made five evenly spaced petals. Take a few stitches on the back and trim off the ends of the thread and ribbon.

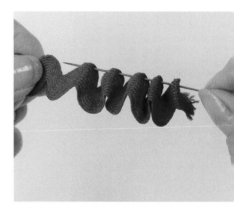

4 To make a rickrack flower, thread the needle, double the thread, and knot both ends. Cut the rickrack through a peak. Fold the cut end to the back and, from the back, bring the needle through the folded rickrack, close to the top of the peak. Continue through five peaks, as shown.

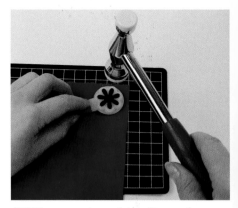

5 Cut the rickrack at the next valley on the same side. From the back, take the needle back through the folded end of the rickrack it came out of in Step 4. Pull the thread up to gather the rickrack into a flower shape.

6 Make a couple of oversewing stitches over the join to close it. Finish the ends securely and trim off thread.

7 Next, punch out fabric flowers from non-fraying fabric with a craft paddle-punch, using a cutting mat to protect your work surface.

sew**SMART**

Make extra flowers to create coordinating accessories, such as a scarf, bag, or gloves. For variation, replace the beads with other embellishments such as sequins, sew-on gems, or buttons.

8 All of the flowers are attached in the same way. Thread a needle, double the thread, and knot the ends together. Position the flower and bring the needle up through the hat, as shown, and the flower to one side of the center. Thread on a bead, then take the needle back down on the other side of the flower center. Repeat a couple of times to hold the flower securely in place.

9 To move to the next flower position, slip the needle through the backs of the knitted stitches on the inside of the hat, ensuring that the thread is not visible on the front. Sew on three or four flowers, and secure the thread on the back. Reknot the thread ends and start the next group of flowers. With this technique, if one flower comes loose, not all of them will be at risk of falling off.

Ribbon pillow

An interesting effect is achieved where the sheer ribbons cross the patterned fabric of this glamorous silk pillow that would lend an air of opulence to any living room. Choose a medium-value thread that will coordinate with all of the ribbons to avoid having to rethread the sewing machine to sew each ribbon.

Materials

- 13½ x 25¼ in. (34 x 64 cm) rectangle of patterned silk fabric
- Selection of satin and organza ribbons in colors to coordinate with the silk, each 26½ in. (67 cm) long and in varying widths from ⅜ in. (9 mm) to 1 in. (25 mm)
- Sewing threads to match ribbons
- 14½-in. (36-cm) square pillow form
- Four tassels with cord loops of equal length
- Sewing machine

Techniques

- Ribbons, page 90

1 Arrange the ribbons across the length of the fabric. When you are happy with the arrangement, pin each in place at the top edge only. The striped fabric is used as a guide to help stitch the ribbons on straight. If you are using plain fabric, mark guide lines on the fabric with an air-erasable fabric marker.

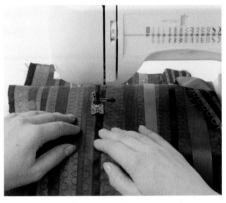

2 Stitch each piece of ribbon to the fabric. Pinning in place can distort the ribbon, so sew short sections at a time, stopping with the needle down in the fabric to straighten the next section. Stitch down one side, close to the edge. Then go back to the top and stitch down the other edge in the same direction as before.

3 When all the ribbons are sewn on, trim the ends protruding beyond the edge of the fabric. With the right sides facing, fold the rectangle of fabric in half lengthwise and lightly press the fold.

4 Position the loop end of a tassel against the fold, with the top aligned with the raw edge of the fabric. Machine stitch across the loops a little under ¾ in. (2 cm) from the raw edge to hold them in place. Attach another tassel opposite.

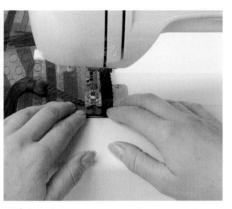

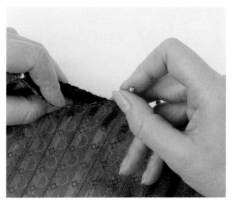

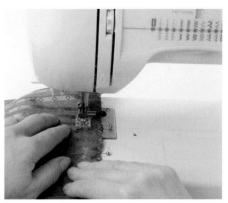

5 Attach two more tassels to opposite corners, positioning the loops ¾ in. (2 cm) from the short edge and against the raw long edge.

6 Carefully pin the two short ends of the rectangle together, matching the ends of ribbon accurately. Pin one of the other two open sides.

7 Machine stitch along these two sides, taking a ¾ in. (2 cm) seam allowance. Turn the corner and stitch ¾ in. (2 cm) of the third side. Stitch ¾ in. (2 cm) up from the fold on this third side, leaving a 4 in. (10 cm) gap in the center of the third side.

8 Turn the pillow cover right-side out through the opening.

9 Insert the pillow form into the cover through the gap. Be careful not to break the stitches on either side.

10 Turn under the ¾ in. (2 cm) seam allowance on one side of the gap. Lay this side over the other with the folded edge ¾ in. (2 cm) in from the raw edge, and pin in place. Slip stitch the gap closed by hand.

sewSMART

If you use a silk fabric that is prone to fraying, zigzag stitch all around the edges before you start working on this pillow project.

Ideas Gallery embellishments

Whether you add movement to a project with dangling tassels, or apply purchased fabric rose petals to voile fabric, embellishments can add a decorative and elegant touch to the simplest of projects.

➤ **Adding an overcheck to fabric** can be done by topstitching ribbon onto a background fabric to create a striped or overcheck effect. Red and green ribbons in different widths are stitched to the background with red thread. Purchased ribbon roses are stitched on at the point where some of the ribbons intersect.

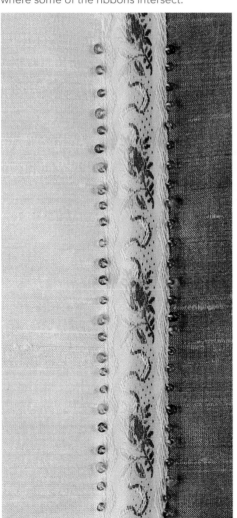

◄ **Decorating with ribbon and bead;** the seam joining these two contrasting silk fabrics has been covered with a strip of pretty woven ribbon. Simply pin the ribbon in place and secure to the ground fabric by backstitching the mixed lilac and pink seed beads by hand.

⋀ **Joining ribbons to make fabric** is a great way to create a unique look. A variety of ribbons in different textures and colors are satin-stitched together to form this fabric, with each subsequent ribbon slightly overlapping the last.

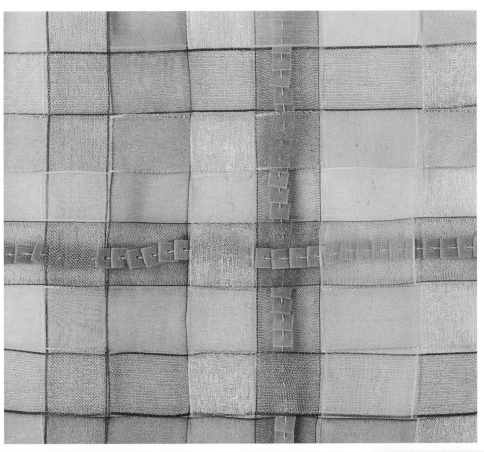

◄ **Weaving ribbons to make fabric**
different-colored sheer ribbons in various
widths are woven together, creating new
hues where the layers overlap. Strung
square sequins are woven through at
intervals to add some extra visual interest.

▲ **Manipulate ribbon** by machine sewing a series of deep tucks in
it, wrong sides together, to provide this unique look. Open out the
tuck and flatten the loop, so the fold aligns with the seam. Lift the
free edges of the loop and bring them toward the center of the
seam, catching them up with a hand stitch. Finish by sewing a
button at the center.

◄ **Purchased fabric rose petals** are applied to the background
fabric, which has been gathered slightly underneath each petal to
add texture and emphasize the dual-colored fabric. Thread a
needle with embroidery floss and knot the end. Starting from the
back, make several small gathering stitches, ending on the front of
the work. Draw up the thread and pass it through a petal. Work a
French knot to hold the petal in place, ending the thread by taking
short stitches on the wrong side.

◄ **Adding a purchased motif** to the back pocket of a pair of jeans proves that good embellishment does not need to be sophisticated and dressy. This patch adds an understated decoration to a casual garment.

⋀ **Piping in vibrant suede** is inserted between the contrasting panels of this project, defining the joins between the fabrics.

⋀ **Embellishing a purchased motif** can add a creative touch. This beaded star is given a tail made from short lengths of ribbons. Secure the ribbons together with a few stitches at one end before tucking them beneath the motif. Stitch around the edge of the star to attach it to the background fabric. Trim the ribbon ends.

Rickrack creates a lovely scalloped effect when it is stitched to the underside of an edge, collar, or hem. Position it just underneath the edge and topstitch it close to the edge of the fabric.

Braids can be used to add interest to the edge of a project. Stitched very close to the edge, this velvet flower trim is wide enough to break up the edge of the project and create a more interesting line.

Multiple lines of piping can be used to make a decorative edge. Lay two rows of piping close together and stitch to secure. Lay the third length next to the second and repeat the stitching process. Join the multiple piping to the project in the usual way, using the stitching line closest to the raw edges of the piping as a sewing guide.

Beading

Beads have fascinated us for thousands of years and still today our eyes are drawn to these small treasures. Widely appreciated for their decorative value, beads are now available in an endless range of sizes, colors, finishes, and base materials, including metal, glass, wood, bone, clay, nuts, seeds, and plastic. From mass-produced beads to unique handmade ones, beads can transform the simplest clothing and home accents into works of art.

Choosing beads

When choosing beads, you can either select them for color or just to add texture and sparkle. Make sure that the beads are not too heavy for the fabric to be used. If the project will be laundered, check that the beads are suitable for washing.

Types of beads

Some widely available types of beads are shown below.

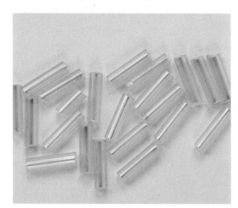

Pale, opalescent bugle beads are available in different lengths and colors.

Color-lined seed beads have a core color and a clear or contrasting outer layer.

Metallic delica beads are ideal for fringing and bead embroidery.

Tiny seed beads work well in bead embroidery, because they can be used to create intricate motifs.
Larger seed beads can add impact, but make sure they are not too heavy.

Feature beads add detail; there are many to choose from. Top, left to right: crystal bead, tiny cut glass flower bead, frosted glass flower bead, diamanté gem. Bottom: Flat, faceted glass flower bead.

Sequins come in various shapes and a variety of colors: look for unusual ones like these pale green squares.

Beaded embroidery

When working bead embroidery on fabric, match the thread color to the fabric rather than to the beads so it will show up less. All of the following stitches are worked in the conventional way; they simply have beads added to them.

Blanket stitch

You can use bugle beads, shown below, and seed beads with blanket stitch (see page 16).

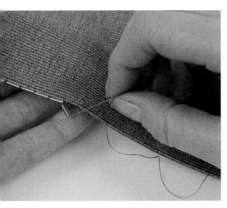

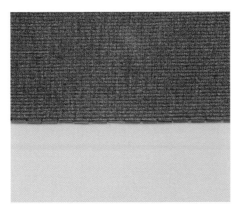

1 Pick up a bead, then from back to front, take the needle through the very edge of the fabric the length of the bead away from where it came out. Take the needle through the loop of thread after the bead and pull gently so that the bead sits flat against the fabric.

2 Beaded blanket stitch makes a glittering edge trim on a project.

sewSMART

To attach beads more securely, work a cross stitch through each bead instead of a single thread. Bring your needle up at the bottom of the bead on one side, cross the thread through the bead to the top of the other side and bring the needle down through the fabric. Continue, bringing the needle back up through the fabric at the opposite top of the bead and then cross the thread through to the bottom of the other side of the bead and finish the cross stitch, taking a few stitches on the back to secure.

Lazy daisy stitch

The number of beads on each lazy daisy will vary, depending on how large you want the finished flower to be.

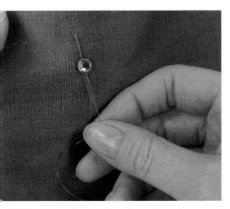

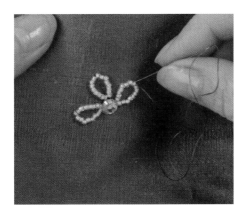

1 Sew on a larger bead, such as the sparkling diamanté gem shown above, to make a center for the flower.

2 Work lazy daisy petals around the center, picking up approximately 16 seed beads on each loop of thread. Without any beads on the thread, make a tiny stitch over the end of each loop.

3 Continue adding beaded petals around the center in the same way. Add as many lazy daisy flowers as desired to your project.

Double-feather stitch

Pick up an even number of beads for each loop of double-feather stitch (see page 19).

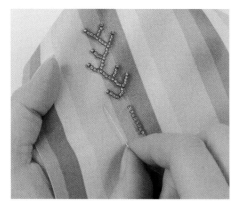

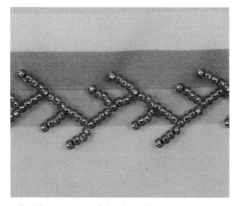

1 Eight seed beads are picked up for each loop. Work the stitch exactly as for conventional double-feather stitch, starting each new stitch between the fourth and fifth beads of the previous stitch.

2 The weight of the beads makes this stitch ideal for embellishing the lower edge of a garment.

Straight stitch

This simple stitch can be used to fill in the center of a beaded motif or just scattered over fabric to add sparkle.

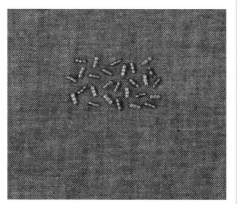

1 Bring the needle up through fabric and pick up three beads. Take the tip of the needle down beyond the third bead so that the line of beads lies flat on the fabric.

2 A single-color bead, or a variety of colors (two are used above) work well with this straight stitch.

Backstitch

The small backstitch (see page 17) allows you to create intricate beaded designs.

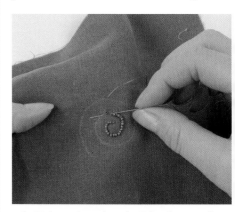

1 Pick up three beads. Take the needle down at the end of the third bead. Bring it up a stitch length beyond the line of beads and repeat the process.

2 When the motif is complete, take the needle through all the beads, pulling very gently, so they will sit neatly in line.

3 Variegated-color beads add extra interest to a beaded motif.

Couching

Straight or wandering lines of beads are best made using couching (see page 19).

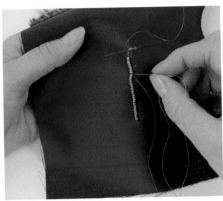

sewSMART

Visit your local bead shop and look for a flat thread called C-Don. This thread is both firm and yet slightly elastic, which makes it very durable. It comes in a selection of basic, neutral colors that will blend with many different fabrics and types of beads.

1 Pick up 20–30 beads. Push the needle through the fabric above the line of beads and loop the thread around it to hold the line taut while you couch it. The thread you use to couch has no beads on it. Make the couching stitches between every third and fourth bead, so that they slip between the beads and disappear.

2 Machine-made beads (as used above) will produce neater lines of couching than more irregularly shaped handmade beads.

Fringing

This is a very simple technique, and yet it produces spectacular results. Fringes can be long or short, colorful or muted; it depends on your project and your own sense of color.

1 Cut a piece of low-tack tape the length of the fringed edge. Make evenly spaced marks on one edge of the tape to establish the distance between the strands of fringe. Stick this tape to the back edge of the fabric. Bring the needle out through the edge of the fabric right at the first marked point. Pick up the beads for one strand of fringe.

2 Skipping the last bead, take the needle back up through the rest. Pull until the first bead lies next to the edge of the fabric. Take the needle back through the fabric. Bring it out at the next marked point and repeat the process. Fringing "grows" surprisingly quickly, so it can be quicker to work a fringed edge than you might think.

Purchased trim

Adding a purchased trim is a very quick and easy way to customize a purchased garment. Trims are available in a wide range of designs and colors, so you can easily find something to suit your needs.

Beaded trim

Follow these steps to add beaded trim to clothing.

1 Pull some beads off the trim thread, to start with a complete pattern repeat; leave the thread ends hanging free. Use a fine sewing needle and sewing thread to match the trim thread. Attach the trim with a form of backstitch: Bring the needle up beside the trim, take a backstitch over it, and pull the thread to slip it between two beads. Bring the needle to the front again farther along the trim, and repeat.

2 When the trim is securely attached, thread a needle with the ends of the bead trim thread, take them to the back of the fabric, and secure them with a couple of small stitches. Beads do not need to be confined to evening wear; a whimsical beaded trim in pastel colors can add panache to an old pair of jeans.

Fringe trim

Follow these steps to add beaded fringe trim to a hem.

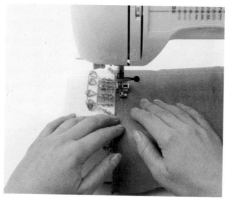

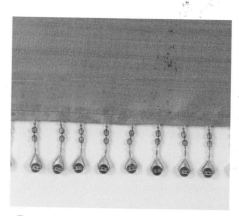

1 Turn under and press a double hem slightly wider than the fabric or ribbon band along the top of the fringe. Open the first fold of the hem and pin the band to it on the right side of the fabric. Using a zipper foot, machine stitch the band to the hem, stitching close to the fringed edge.

2 Fold the hem up and, working on the right side of the fabric and using the marks on the machine bed to guide you, machine stitch close to the top of the hem position, stitching the top of the band in position at the same time.

3 Purchased beaded fringe trim works equally well on home furnishing items or wearable accessories.

Beaded tote

Deceptively easy to make, this charming tote provides an ideal base for bead embroidery. Look for medium-weight felt, so that the bag will be substantial enough to withstand some use. Its non-fray quality means that the edges can be trimmed with pinking shears, adding another decorative detail.

Materials

- Two 9 x 9 in. (22 x 22 cm) pieces of felt
- Air-erasable fabric marker
- Scissors
- Selection of beads
- Beading needle
- Beading thread to match felt
- 8½ x 2 in. (21.5 x 5 cm) strip of felt for base gusset
- Two 8¼ x 2 in. (21 x 5 cm) strips of felt for side gussets
- Two 13 x 1 in. (33 x 2.5 cm) strips of felt
- Sewing thread to match felt
- Pinking shears
- Sewing machine

Techniques

- Lazy daisy stitch, page 107
- Double feather stitch, page 19
- Straight stitch, page 16
- Basic couching, page 19

1 Trim a wedge-shape strip off each side of the two pieces of felt so they narrow to 7 in. (17 cm) wide at the top edge, as shown above. Work beading on one piece, keeping the embroidery ⅝ in. (1.5 cm) away from the edges. Follow the design above or choose a desired motif.

2 With wrong sides facing, machine stitch one side gusset strip to each end of the base gusset strip, taking a ½ in. (1 cm) seam allowance and starting and stopping the stitching ½ in. (1 cm) from the edges. Pull the ends of thread through to the wrong side and knot them.

3 Pin the joined strips to the back piece of the bag. Align the joins with the bottom corners of the back and the raw ends with the top edge.

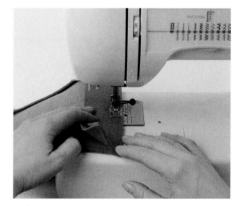

4 Machine stitch the pieces together, taking a ½ in. (1 cm) seam allowance. Stitch up one side from the join, then stitch across the bottom, and finally stitch the last side.

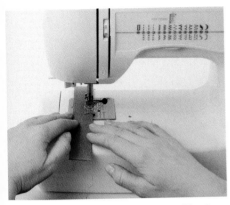

5 Stay stitch around the edges of both handle pieces, stitching ¼ in. (6 mm) in from the edges.

6 Trim the edges of the handles with pinking shears, cutting as close to the edge of the fabric as possible.

7 Pin a handle to the top edge of the front and the other to the back. Position each end of the handle 1 in. (2.5 cm) in from the edge of the bag pieces, with 1⅜ in. (3.5 cm) overlapping the top edge of the bag. Machine stitch the handles to the bag pieces with a rectangle of stitching.

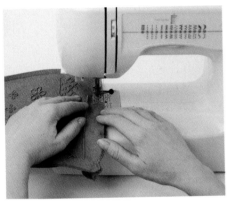

8 Stitch the front of the bag to the free edges of the gusset in the same way as for Step 4.

9 Trim all the seamed edges with the pinking shears.

sewSMART

Beading can lend instant glamour to many projects and it has become very fashionable, so you will easily find a good selection of beaded trims to choose from. Most can be stitched directly to the fabric surface using a thread that will blend in, or with an invisible nylon thread. Beaded fringing comes attached to tape or ribbon that can be stitched to the item.

Beaded fringe scarf

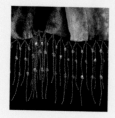

A deep border of beaded fringing accents this hand-painted velvet scarf, heightening its luxurious appearance. The beads have been carefully selected to reflect the sheen and sensuous quality of the velvet.

Materials

- Size 10 seed beads in light and dark shades of your preferred color
- Fire-polished beads in a contrasting color
- Beading needle
- Beading thread to match scarf
- Purchased fabric scarf

Techniques

- Fringing, page 109

1 Bring the needle through the edge of the scarf where the trim is to start. Pick up 7 light beads, 1 fire-polished bead, 20 light, 1 fire-polished, 5 light, 1 dark, 1 light, 2 dark, 1 light, 3 dark, 1 light, 4 dark, 1 light, 5 dark beads. Skipping the last bead, take the needle back through the string; emerge after the first fire-polished bead, as shown.

2 Pick up 8 light beads; then, from front to back, make a tiny stitch through the scarf ½ in. (1 cm) along the edge.

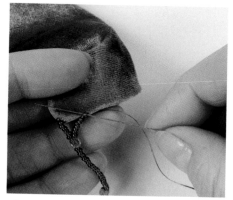

3 Take the needle back through the last bead, ready to begin the next section of fringe.

4 Pick up 15 light beads, 1 fire-polished bead, 5 light, 1 dark, 1 light, 2 dark, 1 light, 3 dark, 1 light, 4 dark, 1 light, and 5 dark beads. Skipping the last bead, take the needle back up through the string and through the bead mentioned in Step 3.

5 Make another tiny stitch through the edge of the scarf in the same place as the stitch made in Step 2. Bring the needle through the last bead again as in Step 3. Repeat Steps 1–5 until the whole edge is fringed. Secure the thread with several short stitches on the wrong side and clip.

Ideas Gallery beadwork

Beading can lend instant glamour to many projects and make them very fashionable. Even the smallest craft shops stock a number of different types of beads.

➤ **Emphasize fabric patterns** with beads by adding coordinating seed and bugle beads interspersed with plain lines of embroidery along the edges of the stripes.

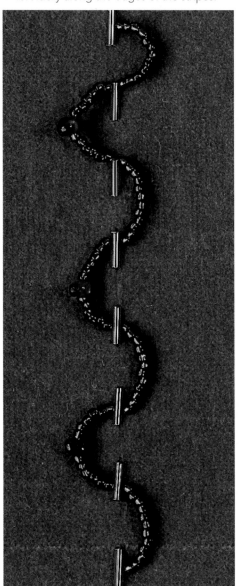

◄ **Decorate plain fabric** with a band of beading. This heavy velvet can support the weight of the many bugle and seed beads on this laced running stitch.

⋀ **Use the design of printed fabric** as a guide for beading. The decorative borders on the edge of the stripes and the tiny rosebuds on this printed fabric are beaded with seed beads in matching colors.

➤ **Use beads to add weight** to fabric by feather stitching different colored small seed beads in stripes along a piece of plain silk. Several rows together at the bottom of a project will add weight, which is useful for a window blind or skirt hem.

◄ **Decorate knitwear** with beaded embellishments. Purchased beaded flower shapes are sewn onto a knitted garment, and simple leaf outlines are added with couched seed beads.

⬈ **Enhance a purchased beaded motif** by adding small seed beads after the motif is stitched in position. These beads suggest the flight path of the sequin dragonfly.

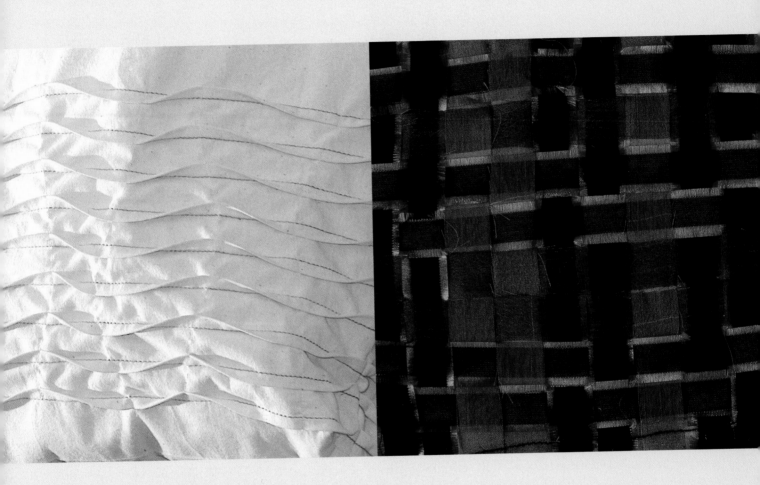

Manipulating Fabric

Although there are more wonderful and interesting fabrics available today than ever before, it can be very satisfying to create your own unique cloth by changing the surface of a fabric. From weaving to gathering, pintucking to distressing and quilting, you'll enjoy using the techniques shown in the following pages to create your own one-of-a-kind wearables and unique accessories.

Treatments and techniques

You can use a variety of techniques and treatments to add texture to your fabric, many of which can alter and distort the surface of the fabric so they are generally best for use on projects you make from scratch rather than on purchased items.

Gathers

Gathers are a classic way of adding fullness to fabric. Because the technique involves sewing over multiple layers of cloth, it is best suited for projects made from light- or mediumweight fabrics.

Machine gathers

Follow these steps to do machine gathering.

1 Set your sewing machine to the longest straight stitch. Stitch two lines along the edge to be gathered, one each side of the seam line. Secure all of the threads at one end by tying them. At the other end, take the top thread from each line of stitching and pull gently, easing the gathers to desired length.

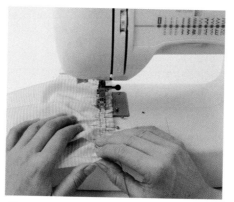

2 To attach gathered fabric to a flat piece, pin the two pieces together with right sides facing, aligning raw edges. Check that the gathers are evenly spaced. With the gathered fabric uppermost, stitch the layers together along the seam line between the two lines of gathers.

3 Pull out all the gathering threads. Depending on the final width of the gathered fabric in relation to the width of the flat piece, the resulting frill can be soft, as shown above, or full.

> ## sewSMART
>
> It is possible to gather heavier fabrics on the machine using an advanced sewing technique. On the wrong side of the fabric, lay a very thin cord over the gathering line and sew a wide zigzag stitch over it while being very careful not to catch the fibers of the cord. After applying the cord, hold the fabric right side toward you and gently pull the cord to form gathers.

Hand gathers
Follow these steps to gather by hand.

1 Thread a long, thin hand-sewing needle with a long length of sewing thread, double it, and knot the end. Take basting stitches along the edge to be gathered within the seam allowance, and keep the stitches as even as possible.

2 Pull the gathers up as for Machine gathers Step 1 (see page 120) and secure the end with two small backstitches. To attach the gathered fabric to a flat piece, follow Step 2 of Machine gathers, but stitch just below the gathering line.

Drawn-thread work
This traditional embellishment technique can work very well in contemporary projects and is extremely easy to do. It works best on fairly loose-weave fabrics.

1 Use the point of a pin (a thin one for fine fabrics, a thicker one for heavier fabrics) to carefully lift a single fiber close to the raw edge. Gently pull on the fiber to pull it completely out.

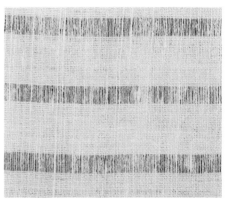

2 Repeat the process to make a pulled-thread band the required width. Drawn-thread work can be done either lengthwise or widthwise and the band can be edged with hand stitching to secure it.

Pintucks
Pintucks are another traditional method of embellishing fabric that can be used to good effect on contemporary, as well as classic, projects.

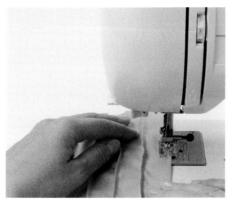

1 Fold and press the fabric along the line of the first pintuck. Stitch a line the required depth in from the folded edge. Use a point on the presser foot of the sewing machine to use as a width guide. The inside edge of the presser foot runs along the folded edge of the fabric. Open the fabric flat and measure from the folded edge to where the fold line of the next pintuck will be. Mark the fabric at this point; then fold, press, and stitch it as before. Repeat the process until all the pintucks have been made.

2 Strictly speaking, a pintuck is a tuck less than 1/8 in. (3 mm) wide: Anything wider is just a tuck.

sewSMART

Fabric often has a tendency to distort when sewing pintucks. To keep the edges square, press and sew them one at a time.

Weaving

Interesting fabrics can be created with weaving. Ribbon is ideal; it is very varied and the long edges are finished, but fabric strips can also be used for a more rustic look.

Shirring elastic

Shirring elastic is available in a limited range of colors, so choose the closest match to your fabric.

1 Cut equal lengths of ribbon and pin them face down to an ironing board. Butt each piece to the edge of the previous one and insert a pin at each end, pushing them in at a sharp angle.

2 Thread a strip of cardboard to lift alternate lengths. Slide another ribbon face down along the cardboard, remove it and pin the ribbon in place. Repeat until the whole panel is woven.

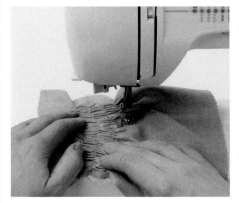

1 Wind the elastic onto the bobbin by hand, keeping the tension even. Use matching regular thread in the top of the machine. Sew straight lines using a medium stitch length.

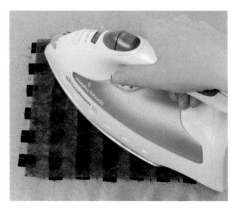

3 Cut a piece of fusible interfacing that is slightly smaller than the woven panel. Lay the interfacing over the panel on the wrong side of the ribbons and press it in place to hold all the ribbons together. Remove all of the pins.

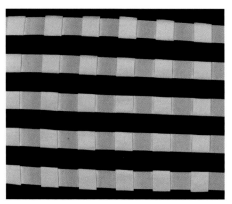

4 Ribbon-woven panels can be used to make glamorous pillow covers and bags. Sheer ribbon or fabric, such as organza, can produce lovely shaded effects.

2 Shirring with elastic is a quick-and-easy way of creating a look similar to traditional smocking.

sewSMART

When using shirring elastic you may need to loosen the tension on the bobbin case; the greater the tension, the more the fabric will be gathered by the elastic. In general, set the stitch length to a medium straight stitch and sew the lines of shirring to your fabric, as required.

Fraying

This technique can be used as an informal edge treatment. Shot fabrics—where warp and weft threads are different colors—produce an attractive effect when the edges are frayed.

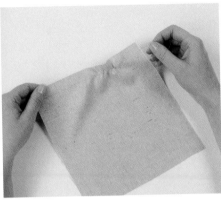

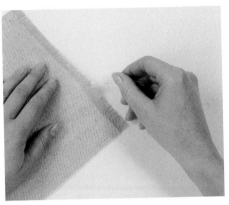

1 Pull out a single thread to establish the straight edge of the fabric. Cut along the resulting line with scissors.

2 Pull out enough threads along the edge of the fabric to create a frayed edge of the required depth.

3 A plain-fabric scarf can be given a delicately fringed edge using this technique.

Distressing

These techniques can add interesting texture and detail to fabric projects and are great tools in any sewer's repertoire.

Melting

This can be done on man-made fibers only. The effects will vary from fabric to fabric, so be sure to experiment with scrap pieces before working on a project. If you melt the fabric too much, it will become very stiff and brittle and you will probably make holes, which may even create the effect you are trying to achieve.

1 Use a craft heat gun on a heat-proof surface (a metallic ironing board cover is ideal) to gently melt sections of fabric.

2 Melting can give plain voile curtains an unusual and contemporary look.

Pulling the weave apart

Do this only on a loose-weave fabric. The outcome will vary slightly, depending on the fabric you use. The effect is rather like drawn-thread work, but fibers are not removed.

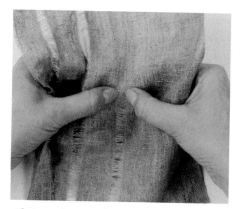

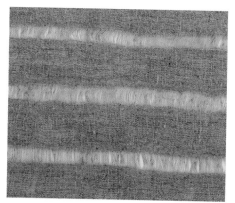

1 Long fingernails are an asset for this technique. Use them to gently ease the threads apart, pushing them aside so that they bunch up along the edges of the open band of threads. This can be hard work, depending on the fabric, so try it on a small project.

2 As with drawn-thread work, the weave can be pulled apart along the warp or the weft threads.

Quilting

Quilting has traditionally been used to make cloth more substantial and much warmer. Similar to other time-honored techniques, such as patchwork, it was often worked by hand, but today your sewing machine can be used to speed up the process.

Assembling layers

The more neatly the layers are assembled, the better your final quilting results will be, so take time to do this well.

1 Lay the backing fabric on a flat work surface; preshrunk muslin is shown above. Lay the batting on top of it, carefully aligning the raw edges and making sure that the backing does not crease. Lay the top fabric right side up on the batting.

2 Pin the three layers together and baste them together, working in horizontal and vertical lines spaced 4 in. (10 cm) apart. Keep the fabrics fairly flat on the work surface. The basting threads will be removed once the quilting is complete.

Machine quilting

Quick-and-easy quilting can be done on a sewing machine.

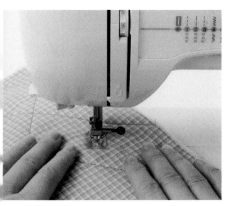

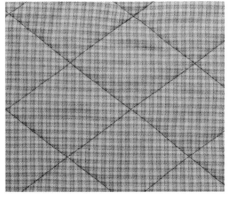

1 Baste the layers together and mark the lines you want to quilt on the fabric with an air-erasable fabric marker. Set the stitch length to a slightly longer than normal stitch and machine stitch over the drawn lines.

2 A simple diamond pattern can be used effectively on a patterned fabric.

Tied quilting

This is a simple technique where tufts of thread provide decorative detail, as well as anchor the layers of fabric together.

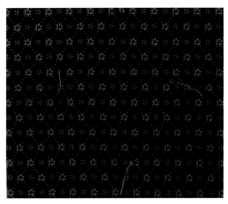

1 Thread a crewel needle with a length of embroidery floss. Take the needle down through all three layers of a quilt sandwich. Pull the thread through to leave a short tail and then take the needle back up again, close to where it came out.

2 Tie the ends of the floss in a secure, flat square knot, and trim them to the required length.

3 Knots can be made at regular intervals, placed randomly, or positioned to complement the design of a patterned fabric, as shown above with this diamond.

Pintucked carryall

This sturdy everyday bag will come in handy for carrying anything from groceries to your beachside essentials. The effects of light and shadow enhances the pleated detail and add visual interest. Made from natural, undyed fabrics this tote will easily withstand frequent machine washing.

Materials

- 59 x 16 in. (150 x 40 cm) rectangle of muslin
- 35 x 16 in. (89 x 40 cm) rectangle of cotton canvas
- Brown topstitching thread
- Cream sewing thread
- Scissors
- Sewing machine

Techniques

- Pintucks, page 121
- Making ties, page 147

1 Fold the muslin strip in half widthwise and press a fold. Above it, measure up 2 in. (5 cm) and press a fold parallel to the first. Using brown topstitching thread, set the machine to a slightly longer straight stitch and, with the outer edge of the foot against the pressed fold, sew a tuck. Mark 1¼ in. (3 cm) up from line of stitching, press a fold and sew another tuck. Repeat to make nine tucks on each side of first fold.

2 Working at right angles to the pleats and using cream sewing thread, sew six lines over the pleats using a medium straight stitch. Space the lines evenly across the fabric, stitching the pleats in alternate directions to create waves in them. If pleats are facing "up," then start the line of stitching at the top edge of the pleat: If they are facing "down," start at the line of topstitching.

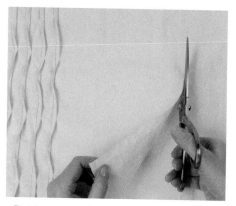

3 Measure and mark 17½ in. (44 cm) up at either end of the last fold. Draw a straight line, parallel to the fold at this point, and then cut off any excess fabric.

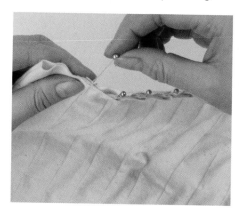

4 With right sides facing, fold the fabric along the first fold line and pin the edges together, as shown above, matching the pleats carefully. Sew down the sides, taking a ⅝ in. (1.5 cm) seam allowance.

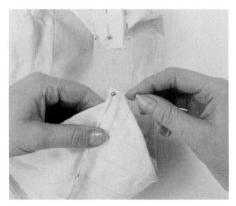

5 Open out the bottom corners. Match the side seam to the fold across the bottom, and put in pins below the first tuck to pin the corners into a flat point.

6 Measure 1³⁄₈ in. (3.5 cm) down from the point and make a mark. At this mark, sew a line across the point at right angles to the side seam.

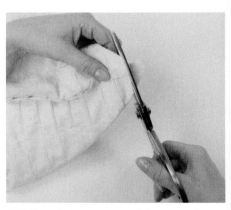

7 Cut off the top part of the point above the line of stitching.

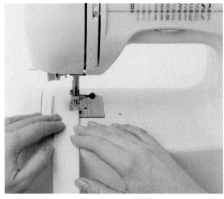

8 To make the handles, cut a 16 x 4³⁄₄ in. (40 x 12 cm) strip from each of the pieces of muslin cut away in Step 3. Make the handles as shown for Making ties, Steps 1–4 on page 147, leaving short ends raw.

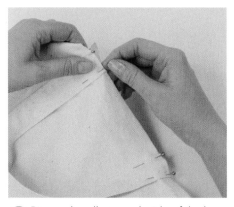

9 Pin one handle to each side of the bag with each end 4 in. (10 cm) from a side seam, aligning the ends with the raw top edge of the bag. Machine baste over the handle ends to hold them in place.

10 To make the lining, fold the piece of canvas in half widthwise and press the fold. Sew the sides together taking a ⅝ in. (1.5 cm) seam allowance, but leaving a 4 in. (10 cm) gap halfway down on one side. Follow Steps 5–7 to square off the bottom corners. With right sides facing, slip the muslin bag inside the lining.

11 Pin the raw edges together around the top then sew them, taking a ⅝ in. (1.5 cm) seam allowance and stitching around twice. Pull the muslin bag out of the lining and turn the whole thing right side out through the opening in the side of the lining. Slip stitch the opening closed.

12 Push the lining down inside the bag, ensuring that the corners match. Press the top edge thoroughly. Top stitch in cream thread next to the top edge of the bag.

Textured scarf

Drawn-thread work is the technique used to create this attractive scarf. To introduce additional color and texture, ribbon and frayed fabric has been woven through the gaps, and glass beads add an elegant touch.

Materials

- 78 x 13½ in. (198 x 34 cm) length of pea green, plain weave, viscose fabric
- Two 14½ x 2⅝ in. (37 x 6.5 cm) pieces of aqua silk
- Four 14½ x 1 in. (37 x 2.5 cm) lengths of green organza ribbon
- Large-eye, blunt-point needle
- Two 14½ x ⅝ in. (37 x 1.5 cm) lengths of green organza ribbon
- Two 14½ x ½ in. (37 x 1 cm) lengths of turquoise double-sided satin ribbon
- Two 78 x ⅝ in. (198 x 1.5 cm) lengths of green organza ribbon
- Machine sewing thread to match the green organza ribbon
- Flat green disk beads
- Blue seed beads
- Beading needle
- Green beading thread

Techniques

- Drawn-thread work, page 121
- Fraying, page 123

sewSMART

If drawing threads and threading ribbons through them is difficult to see clearly, try wearing a pair of reading glasses in a magnification level that allows you to see and count the threads easily.

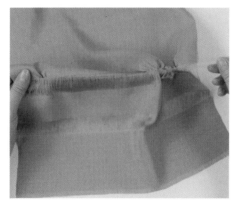

1 Draw out a 1 in. (2.5 cm)-wide band of threads, 2⅝ in. (6.5 cm) up from one short edge of the fabric. Draw the next band 1½ in. (4 cm) farther up the fabric and make it 1¼ in. (3 cm) wide.

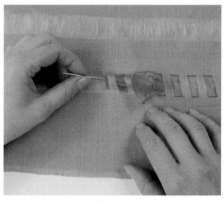

2 Thread a length of the 1 in. (2.5 cm) wide ribbon into the needle. Weave the ribbon through the first band of drawn threads, over and under a ⅜ in. (1cm)-wide section of threads each time.

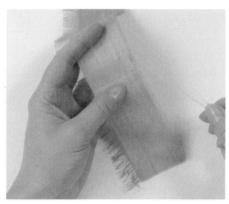

3 Fray the long edges of both strips of aqua silk evenly, until the central piece of fabric is 1¼ in. (3 cm) wide.

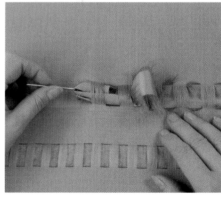

4 Thread one strip into the needle and weave it through the next band of threads, over and under ¼ in. (1.5 cm) apart.

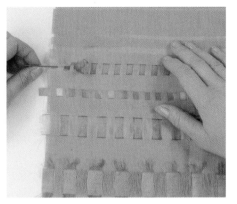

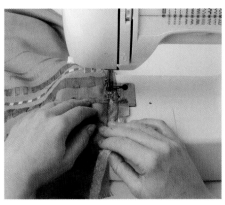

5 Use the point of the needle to pull the frayed edges of the silk through the drawn threads, so that they hang vertically up and down from the edges of the fabric. Repeat steps 1–5 on both ends of the scarf.

6 Continue drawing bands of thread from the fabric and then threading short lengths of ribbon through them, using the photograph on page 130 and the width of the ribbon for guidance.

7 To finish the sides of the scarf, trim the long raw edges of the fabric straight, but do not cut off the ends of the threaded ribbons. Pin one 78 in. (198 cm) length of ribbon to one long edge, so that half the ⅝ in. (1.5 cm) width overlaps the edge of the fabric. Start and stop the ribbon 1 in. (2.5 cm) from the short ends of the scarf, folding under ¼ in. (6 mm) of ribbon at each end. Pin carefully over the ends of the woven ribbon. Set the sewing machine to a medium straight stitch and, using the green sewing thread, sew the overlapping edge of the ribbon to the fabric, stitching close to the edge of the ribbon.

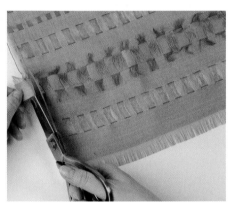

8 Trim the ends of each of the woven ribbons so they are level with the edges of the fabric.

9 Turn over the scarf and fold the free edge of the ribbon over the edge of the fabric and machine stitch it down, sewing over the first line of stitching.

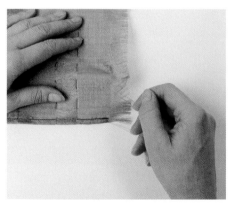

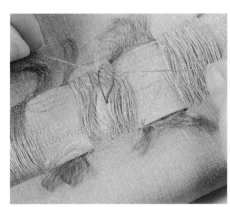

10 Repeat Steps 7–9 for the other side of the scarf. Pull out enough threads to fray the 1 in. (2.5 cm) raw edge at each short end of the scarf.

11 Thread the beading needle, but do not knot the thread end. Bring the needle up through the center of a rectangle of woven aqua silk, between the warp threads. Leave a 4 in. (10 cm) tail of thread at the back. Pick up a disk bead and a seed bead. Skip the seed bead, take the needle back through the disk and the fabric.

12 Tie the ends of thread together in a firm knot on the wrong side of the scarf, ensuring that you don't catch any of the warp threads in the knot. Repeat the process on each rectangle of aqua silk, on both ends of the scarf.

Ruched bolster

This small but sumptuous bolster pillow will lend a soft touch to any room in the home. Dupioni silk is an ideal fabric weight for this project. If it were any heavier, the fabric would not gather so well.

Materials

- Rectangle of dupioni silk fabric measuring 25½ x 20½ in. (65 x 52 cm)
- Air-erasable fabric marker
- Nine 25½ in. (65 cm) lengths of ¼ in. (6 mm) piping cord
- Sewing thread to match fabric
- Two 25½ x 1⅜ in. (65 x 3.5 cm) strips of dupioni silk fabric cut along the straight grain, for end piping
- Two 25½ in. (65 cm) lengths of ⅛ in. (3 mm) piping cord
- Two 18½ x 2⅝ in. (47 x 6.5 cm) strips of dupioni silk fabric cut along the straight grain, for end panels
- Two 1¼ in. (3 cm) self-cover buttons
- Scraps of silk to cover buttons
- Sewing needle
- Sewing machine
- 12 x 4 in. (30 x 10 cm) bolster pillow form

Techniques

- Piping, page 93
- Covering buttons, page 142

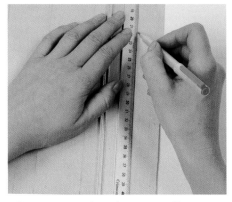

1 Measure and mark a series of lines across the largest piece of silk fabric. Place the first line 1¼ in. (3 cm) from one long edge, then mark eight more parallel lines, each one 2¼ in. (5.5 cm) apart.

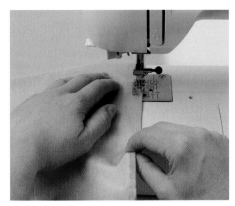

2 Neaten the long edges of the fabric by turning them under ¼ in. (6 mm) twice and machine stitching a narrow double hem.

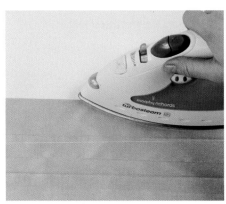

3 Fold the fabric wrong sides together along each marked line and press.

4 On the wrong side of the fabric, lay a length of ¼ in. (6 mm) piping cord along the first pressed crease. At the top, take a few machine stitches along the cord to hold it in place, as shown above, be sure that the cord is lying on top of the pressed crease and make sure that the stitches are within the ⅝ in. (1.5 cm) seam allowance.

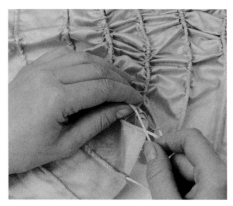

5 Fold the fabric over the cord, so that the cord is tight against the crease. As if you were making piping, and using the zipper foot on the machine, stitch along the side of the cord to encase it in the fabric. Repeat Steps 4–5 at each pressed crease.

6 Pull on the bottom ends of the cords and ruche the fabric along them to half its original length 12¾ in. (32 cm). Be sure to pull evenly on all of the cords at the same time so that the bottom edge of the fabric is completely straight.

7 Once the ruching is complete, machine stitch over the ends of the cords to hold them in place and stop the ruching from unraveling. Cut off the excess cords.

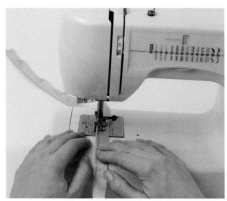

8 Fold the 1¼ in. (3 cm) strip marked in Step 1 under the ruching and leave the other flat. At one end of the bolster cover, lay the folded side over the flat side and pin them so that the ruching on the folded side just covers the ruching on the flat side. Machine stitch over the ends to hold them in place, stitching within the ⅝ in. (1.5 cm) seam allowance. Repeat at the other end.

9 Make up the 25½ in. (65 cm) strips of silk and ⅛ in. (3 mm) piping cord into two lengths of piping. Using the zipper foot on the machine, stitch over one end of the cord to stop it pulling out of the casing. Ruche the fabric over the cord to make a 15¼ in. (38 cm) length of ruched piping. Repeat for the second cord.

10 Starting to one side of the join in the bolster cover, and leaving a short tail, pin and sew the ruched piping to one end of the cover. You will find this easier if you push the ruching up the cord a little, away from the end. Align the raw edges of the piping with the raw edge of the cover and stitch as close to the piping cord as possible. As you reach the starting point, cross the ends of the piping over so that they protrude into the seam allowance and stitch straight over the top of them. Pipe both ends of the cover.

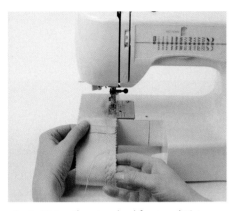

11 Using the standard foot and ⅝ in. (1.5 cm) seam, join the short ends of one 18½ in. (47 cm) strip of silk; press the seam open. Sew three lines of gathering threads along each edge of the circle of fabric, within the seam allowance.

12 Gather one edge of the circle as tightly as possible and tie off the threads. Gather up the other edge to fit one piped end of the bolster cover.

13 With right-sides facing and matching the seams, pin the gathered end-piece to the piped end of the cover. Make sure that the gathers in the end piece are evenly spread.

14 Working on the cover side (so that you can see the line of stitching made when attaching the piping), sew the gathered end to the cover, stitching over the visible line of stitching. Make a second gathered end-piece and sew it to the other end of the cover.

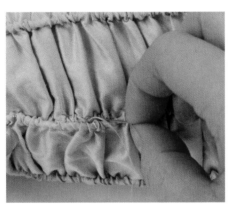

15 Put the bolster pillow form into the cover. Pin the opening closed in the same way as in Step 8. Using doubled thread, firmly slip stitch the opening closed.

16 Cover the buttons according to instructions on page 142 and sew one on each end of the bolster to cover the central gathering. Sew around the edge of the button, slipping the needle through the gathered fabric on the end of the bolster, then catching the fabric on the very edge of the button.

sewSMART

For a touch of glitz you could add a few beads to the fabric circle you cut for covering the two end buttons. Just make sure that all the beads are stitched within the area of the fabric that will be visible after the buttons are stitched to the bolster pillow.

Ideas Gallery manipulating fabric

Textured fabrics add wonderful decorative effects to sewing projects. These techniques can be especially appropriate for enhancing garments or furnishings.

➤ **Two strips of fabric** with curved ends and pinked edges, are gathered along one edge, using two rows of machine gathering. The gathered edge of each strip is then stitched into a gently curved seam. Remove the gathering thread after the seam is secured.

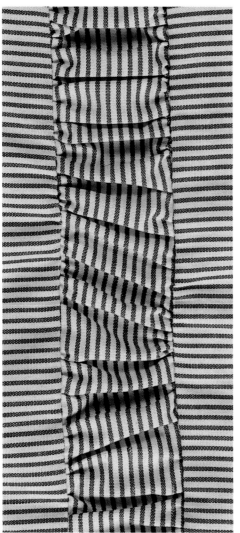

◄ **To create a gathering on two edges,** a strip of fabric cut with the stripes running in one direction is gathered onto flat strips of fabric that are cut with the stripes running in the opposite direction.

⋀ **Variable-width satin stitch** is a simple way to add detail. The width of the satin stitch is adjusted as the leaves and veins are stitched to achieve a sensitive line. The sections between the veins are cut out using sharp-tipped scissors.

Shirring in random directions can be worked with the free-motion machine embroidery technique (see page 29) to create an interesting dimensional surface. Lower the feed dogs on the sewing machine and working with an embroidery foot, stitch spirals at random intervals across the fabric. Stitch curving lines that weave between the spirals to add decoration and texture to the fabric.

Shirring in opposing directions occurs when the fabric is shirred in one direction and again at 90 degrees to the first lines of shirring. All lines are kept equidistant.

Single frayed edges add texture and movement. Strips of a black and cream shot (contrasting color warp and weft threads) silk Dupioni are cut, some lengthwise and some widthwise. One long edge is frayed to expose the contrasting threads. A striped effect can be achieved by stitching the unfrayed edges of each strip to a base fabric in rows using zigzag stitch, ensuring that the adjacent strip conceals the stitching.

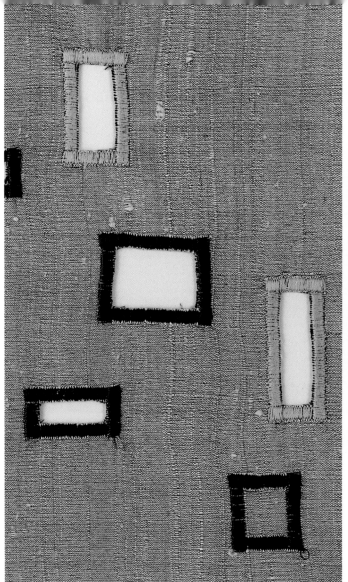

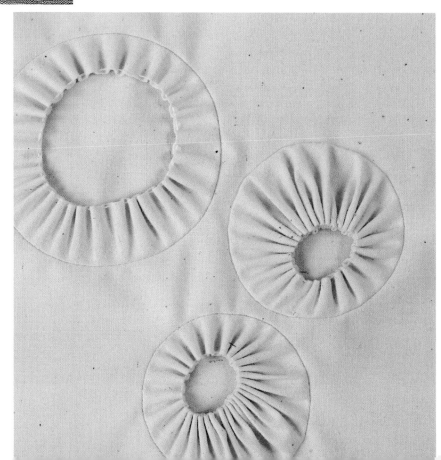

Weaving strips of frayed fabric cut from two different shot fabrics (one sheer) using a rotary cutter and cutting mat. The edges of strips of the opaque fabric are frayed before both strips are woven together in random order.

Satin-stitched edges around holes cut in fabrics make an unusual design. Always do the stitching before cutting the fabric. A wide satin stitch is used to stitch around marked rectangles and the fabric within the stitching area is then cut out using sharp-tipped scissors.

➤ **Gathering the edge of an inner circle** cut in fabric. These "yo-yos" are formed by cutting circles of fabric, and applying them to a piece of the same fabric. Using a fabric marker on the right side of the fabric, draw a small circle within the cut-out circle. The distance between the drawn circle and the outer edge should be less than the radius of the inside circle. The drawn line will be the perimeter of the finished yo-yo. Gather the inner edge, roll edges of the outer edge and stitch to the background. Finger press raw edge to the front and hand sew a line of gathering stitches close to the fold. Machine-stitch the circle to the background, following the drawn circle. Pull up the gathers and tie off threads securely.

◄ **Shadow quilting** simple leaf shapes. The leaves are bonded to a striped background fabric with fusible web and covered with a layer of organza. The layers are held together with free-motion machine embroidery, which also adds detail to the motifs.

⋏ **Hand quilting stitches** follow the design of the printed fabric.

◄ **With slash quilting,** sew two layers of silk together around the edge, leaving a small gap to insert small scraps and colored fabrics and threads. Equidistant lines of stitching hold the layers together. One side of the silk is then cut between the lines of stitching.

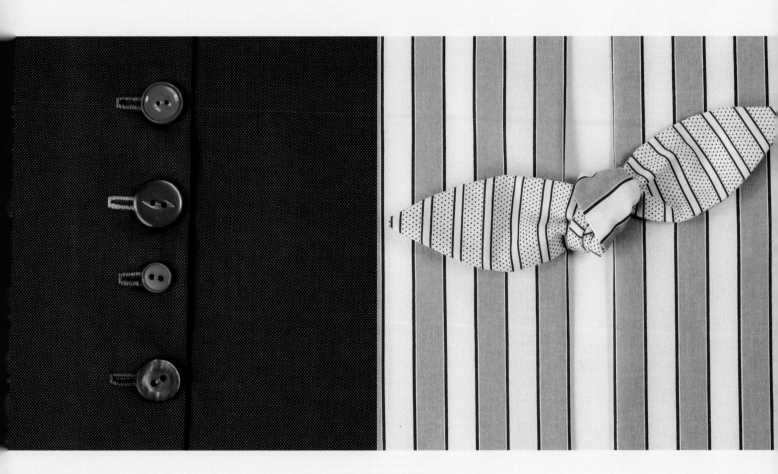

Fastenings

Fastenings play an important role in many sewing projects; although the closure
device is often kept as discreet as possible, there are occasions when the
fastenings can play a decorative as well as a functional role in garments,
accessories, and home furnishings.

Buttons, zippers, and ties

Be sure to consider the wide variety of fastenings and closures that are available today and how they may best be applied to your sewing project. In addition to the ones described in this chapter, snaps and hooks and eyes are available in different sizes and finishes. Use the correct weight fastener to suit your project. Buttons come in a dazzling variety of styles, designs, colors, and sizes—but fabric-covered buttons made using a kit can be a lovely finishing touch.

Covering buttons
Covered-button kits vary, so check the manufacturer's instructions on the ones you buy. The steps below show one of many methods used to cover buttons.

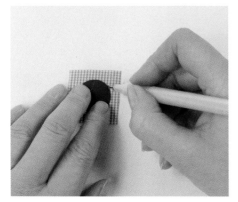

1 Cut out the right size template from the back of the button package. Using a fabric marker, draw around the template onto the right side of the fabric, and cut out the fabric circle.

2 Using doubled sewing thread, work a row of hand gathering stitches around the edge of the fabric circle. Slip the button top onto it and pull the gathering stitches tight. Tie the ends of the threads in a knot.

3 Push the raw edge of the fabric into the top of the button and push the back piece onto the button.

Printed fabric
In this case, fabric with a small printed motif has been used to cover the button. So that you can see the section of print you are cutting out for the button, make a reverse template by cutting the right-sized hole out of a piece of cardboard. If the fabric is thin, like this printed voile, it must be lined to prevent the button showing through. Use the following method, shown at right.

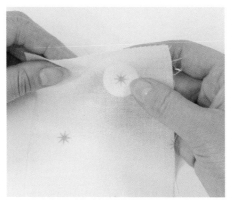

1 Cut the right size circle in plain fabric and position it behind the section of pattern you want to use. Pin it in place then cut it out and cover the button (see above), working with both layers of fabric as one.

2 Make sure you center the motif before pushing the back onto the button.

Beaded buttons

Add sparkle to a button by stitching on beads.

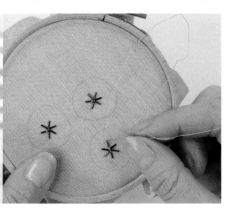

1 With the fabric in an embroidery hoop, mark the number of button circles you need. Six bugle beads and a tiny seed bead are sewn into the middle of the fabric to make simple star shapes.

2 Cut the circles out and use them to cover the buttons (see page 142). The plainest shirt can be livened up with beaded buttons.

Making button loops

Button or rouleau loops make a pretty alternative to buttonholes, provided that they are in keeping with the style of the project. They may be set into a seam at the edge of a piece, or be part of an intricate decorative shape called a frog, which is sewn in place on the outside of a project. Button loops are often seen positioned closely together to make a decorative feature down the back of wedding gowns or other very dressy garments.

Thread loops

These are weaker than machine-stitched buttonholes or rouleau loops, so do not use them if the fabric will be under strain.

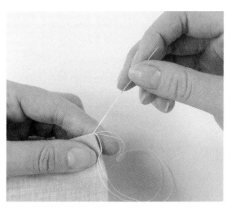

1 Using a strong thread doubled, bring the needle out of the edge of the fabric and in again to make a couple of a loops large enough to go over the button.

2 Work blanket stitch (see page 16) over the looped threads, working from the top down to cover all the loop. Work carefully, so the stitches are flat and even.

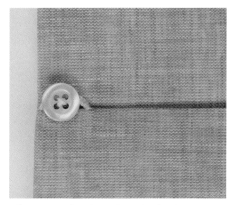

3 Secure the thread on the back. Worked in a color to match the fabric, a thread loop is an almost invisible button fastening.

Rouleau loops

This technique works best on fine fabrics, such as silk or the cotton shirting used below. The seam allowance fills the tubing to create a full, rounded shape. You will need a purchased loop turner, available from fabric stores. Always make a test loop to see how the fabric works into tubing to establish the best seam allowance-to-stitching ratio, and to work out the size loop required to accommodate the button.

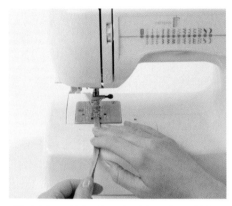

1 Make a ¾ in. (2 cm)-wide strips of bias tape following Steps 1–3 on page 92. Make a separate strip for each loop. With right-sides facing, fold the strip together; sew with a ¼ in. (6 mm) seam allowance.

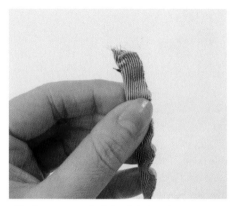

2 Cut one end of the fabric tube in a slant. Thread a loop turner up the tube so the hook appears at the slanted end. Push the latch of the turner through the fabric to hook it securely.

3 Dampen your fingers and ease the fabric tube up over the end of the turner. The tube will turn inside out and the seam allowances will fill the tube firmly.

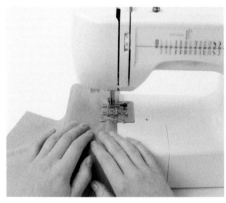

4 Each loop must be big enough to fit the button, plus twice the seam allowance. Pin the loops to the edge of the fabric, aligning ends with the raw edge. Stitch the ends within the seam allowance.

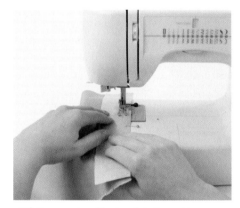

5 Cut a strip of facing fabric and iron lightweight interfacing onto the back. Lay the facing right side down on top of the loops, aligning the raw edges. Sew along the seam, open up the facing and press the seam flat, with the loop ends and seam allowance toward the facing.

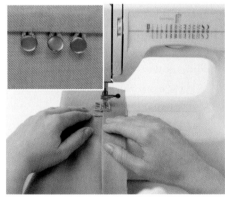

6 Sew along the edge of the facing, ¼ in. (6 mm) from the seam, stitching through the facing, the loop tails, and seam allowances. Fold the facing; press it toward the inside, so that the loops stand out from the finished edge.

Making buttonholes

Buttonholes can be worked by hand, but sewing machines make the process simpler and quicker. A machine-stitched buttonhole has a bar tack at either end, and two close rows of tiny satin stitches. The hole is usually cut manually between the rows of stitching. The length of the buttonhole depends on the shape and size of the button; some machines measure and set it automatically. Always do a test on a scrap of fabric first, because a domed button needs a larger buttonhole than a flat button, even if the diameter is identical. For flat buttons, measure the diameter and add ⅛ in. (3 mm), so the button can slip in and out easily. For domed or other shape buttons, wrap a piece of ribbon over the highest part and pin the ends together. Slip the ribbon off the button and measure from the pin to the halfway point, adding ⅛ in. (3 mm). A row of buttonholes must be equally sized and exactly in line, so mark the positions before you begin. Always reinforce the stitching area with interfacing and stitch fine fabrics using a layer of tear-away stabilizer. Stitch buttonholes in line with the direction of any tension on the fabric, so that they will not gape.

Machine-stitched buttonholes

Many sewing machines have a one-stop buttonhole feature; if you plan on doing even a little dressmaking, this is a very useful feature.

1 Following all the manufacturer's instructions, set up the machine and work the buttonhole.

2 Push the point of a pair of embroidery scissors into the middle of the buttonhole. Using just the points, cut to each end; be careful not to cut the stitches.

3 Machine-stitched button holes look neat and professional.

Hand-stitched buttonholes

Buttonhole stitch is a variation of blanket stitch (see page 16). Work it in the same way, but wind the thread around the needle as shown in Step 3.

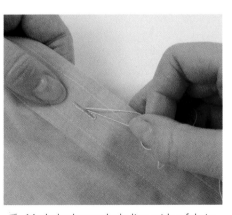

1 Mark the buttonhole line with a fabric marker. Using buttonhole thread, work tiny running stitches right around and ⅛ in. (3 mm) away from this drawn line.

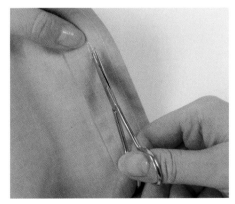

2 Cut along the drawn line with the points of sharp embroidery scissors, being careful not to cut the stitches.

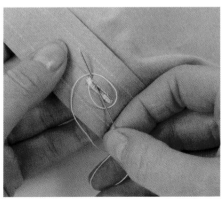

3 Work buttonhole stitch around the edges of the cut, with the stitches close together and covering the running stitches. Fan the stitches neatly at the ends.

In-seam buttonholes

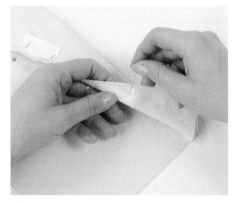

1 For each buttonhole, cut a lightweight fabric stay 1 in. (2.5 cm) wide and 1 in. (2.5 cm) longer than the opening. Pin either side of the seam, centered on the opening.

2 Machine stitch the seam between the marked buttonholes. Trim the stays to the depth of the seam allowance; press the seam open.

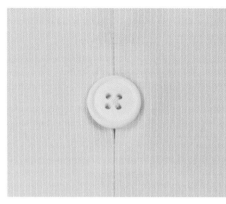

3 You can use in-seam buttonholes as discreet closures for garments and furnishing projects.

Lapped in-seam zipper

A lapped zipper is where one side of the fabric overlaps the zipper to conceal it. You will need a minimum seam allowance of ⅝ in. (1.5 cm) to cover the slider.

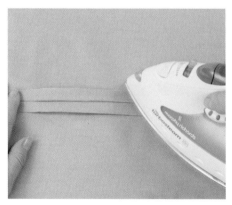

1 Measure the zipper and mark this on the seam. Stitch the seam up to these points; press seam allowances open.

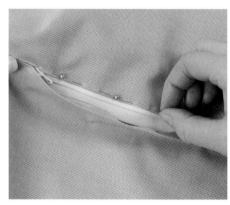

2 Place the zipper behind the slot. Pin the right-hand side to the zipper tape, with the folded edge tight to the teeth.

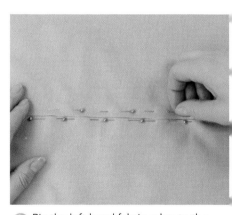

3 Pin the left-hand fabric edge to the tape, butting the folds together and, placing pins ready to remove as you sew.

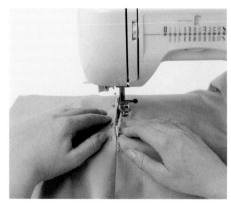

4 With the zipper open, sew down one side. Halfway, with the needle down, lift the foot, close the zipper, finish sewing.

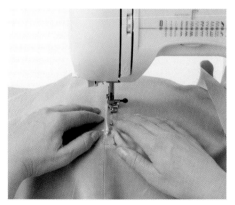

5 With the needle down, pivot the fabric, sew across the base. Sew the other side ⅜ in. (1 cm) from the fold.

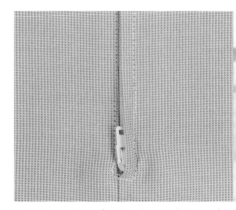

6 Use a zipper foot in the machine and mark a line in air-erasable fabric marker as a guide for stitching, if you prefer.

Making and adding ties

Ties can be smart accents to a project, especially if made from contrasting colored or textured cloth. Always consider how the tie will be used and choose a fabric that can contend with this type of wear. Reinforce lightweight fabrics with interfacing, if necessary. Follow these steps for easy ties.

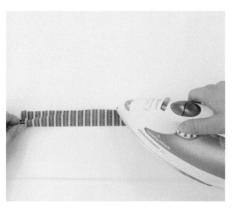

1 Cut a strip of fabric four times the width of the tie and 1½ in. (4 cm) longer. Press ¾ in. (2 cm) at one short end. Wrong sides facing, fold in half lengthwise and press.

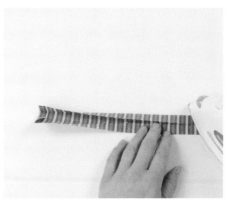

2 Open the strip and press the raw edges to the center.

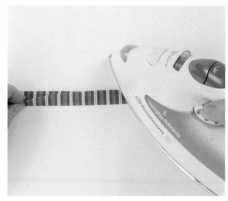

3 Fold the strip in half lengthwise and press it to the finished width.

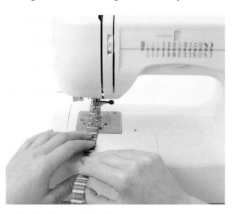

4 Machine stitch all the way around the strip, sewing ⅛ in. (3 mm) in from the edges.

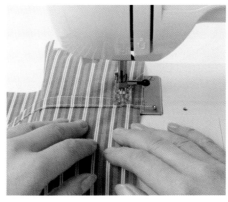

5 Position the tie on the fabric, aligning the raw end with the raw edge of the fabric. Machine stitch over the end of the tie, within the seam allowance.

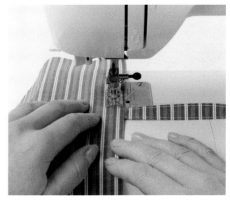

6 Turn under and press a ⅝ in. (1.5 cm) seam allowance. Top stitch the seam ½ in. (12 mm) from the folded edge. Make a second tie, following Steps 1–6.

7 Accurately position the ties on either side of an opening to be sure that they are exactly opposite one another.

sewSMART

Separating zippers are usually centered on the seam. To ensure a straight line of stitching down the length of the zipper on the outside, center a strip of Magic tape over the closed zipper seam and use that as a guide. This is especially helpful if you intend to use heavy topstitching thread to do the final stitching or to finish it by hand with a novelty thread. Be careful not to stitch through the tape.

Decorative button

This gorgeous bead-and-jewel-encrusted button transforms a plain cardigan into an opulent evening jacket. A sprinkling of beads stitched to the garment in a sunburst effect around the button draws the eye toward the central feature.

Materials

- Piece of silk fabric large enough to cover button
- Air-erasable fabric marker
- 4 in. (10 cm) embroidery hoop
- Beading needle
- Beading thread to match fabric
- ⅜ in. (1 cm) cup sequins
- Small seed beads
- Diamanté gems
- ¼ in. (6 mm) cup sequins
- 1½ in. (4 cm) self-cover button
- Sewing needle
- Sewing thread to match garment
- Embroidery floss to match garment

Techniques

- Covering buttons, page 142
- Thread loops, page 143

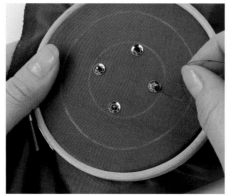

1 Draw the outer button circle on the fabric in a small embroidery hoop. Draw an inner circle centrally, the size of the button. Just inside the inner circle, stitch a ⅜ in. (1 cm) sequin and bead at each point of the compass: Bring the needle up through the fabric, pick up a sequin and a bead. Skip the bead, take the needle back through the sequin and fabric. Continue sewing the bead-topped sequins evenly around the circle.

2 Using the same quartering method, sew a ring of diamanté gems inside the ring of sequins: Stitch through the finding on the back of each gem to attach it. Repeat the technique again, using the same quartering method, to sew a ring of ¼ in. (6 mm) sequins topped with beads inside the ring of diamanté gems.

3 Sew a final diamanté gem into the center of the circle. Cover the button in the usual way (see page 142) and sew onto the garment.

4 Use embroidery floss to make a thread button loop on the edge opposite the button. Be sure that the loop is large enough for the button to pass through.

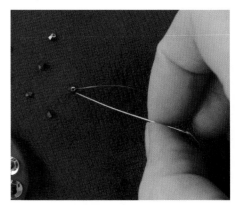

5 Embellish the front of the garment, on either side of the button, with lines of stitched-on beads.

Table runner

Dress up your table when it's not in use with a beautiful silk table runner made in colors to complement your dining room décor. The loop fastening and quirky buttons created from washers not only add decorative detail, but also allow panels to be added to lengthen the runner for use on an extendable table.

Materials

- Template on page 157
- Air-erasable fabric marker
- Approximately 60 in. (150 cm) of silk fabric in various colors
- Sewing thread to complement one of the fabric colors (use this for the embroidery and to stitch all of the pieces together)
- 18 x ¼ in. (6 mm) flat washers
- Lightweight interlining
- Enough cotton sateen lining to back each piece of the runner
- Sewing machine

Techniques

- Machine piecing, page 66
- Rouleau loops, page 144
- Fabric preparation, page 64

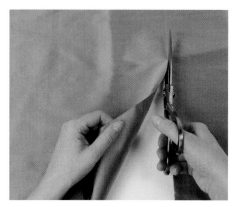

1 Photocopy the piecing diagram on page 156 and adjust it to fit your runner measurements. Mark the pieces on the fabrics, adding ⅝ in. (1.5 cm) seam allowances all around, and cut them out.

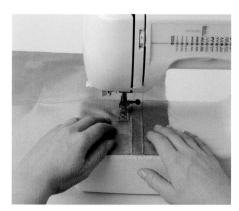

2 Set the sewing machine to satin stitch. Mark a line 1⅝ in. (4 cm) from one edge of a panel, then two more lines, each ⅝ in. (1.5 cm) away. Satin stitch along the lines, adjusting the width of the stitch at random.

3 Join the short pieces to make full-width strips. With the machine on medium straight stitch, sew the pieces together with ⅝ in. (1.5 cm) seam allowance. Press open.

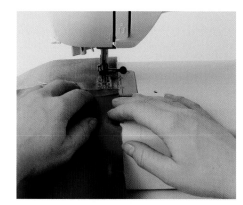

4 Sew the joined strips to the larger pieces in the same way, following your piecing diagram for the central section and two end panels. Press all sections.

5 Make 137 in. (350 cm) of rouleau
tubing in one of the colored silks. At one end loop the rouleau around three times and make a chunky knot. Pull it tight 1½ in. (4 cm) from the end of the rouleau.

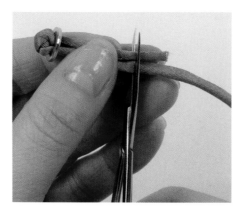

6 Thread on a washer, pushing it up to
the knot. Holding the washer close to the knot, cut the ends of the rouleau 1 in. (2.5 cm) from the washer. Make 18 washer buttons this way.

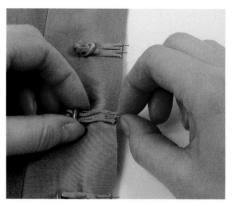

7 Lay nine washer buttons on one end of
each end panel. Position one just inside the seam allowance on each side and space the remaining ones evenly between. Align the raw ends of each button with the raw edge of the fabric and put a pin into each end of the rouleau. Using the sewing machine, baste across the ends of the rouleau, stitching within the seam allowance.

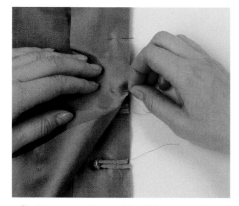

8 Cut a strip the width of the runner by
2½ in. (6 cm) wide. Pin this to the end of the section, pinning it over the ends of the rouleau, so that it covers the buttons.

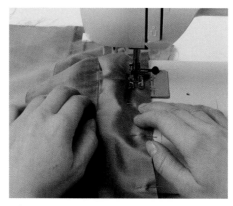

9 Machine stitch the strip to the end of
the panel, taking a ⅝ in. (1.5 cm) seam allowance.

10 Open the strip and press the seam,
with the seam allowance toward the panel.

sewSMART

Tables sizes vary. To work out the size of runner to fit your table use these guidelines:
- This runner is designed to fit a table 39 in. (99 cm) wide by 60 in. (152 cm) long, which extends to 78 in. (198 cm) long.
- The central section of the runner measures 18 x 50 in. (45 x 127 cm) long. The button-on end panels each measure 18 x 20¼ in. (45 x 52 cm), so when they are added, the whole runner measures 18 x 91½ in. (45 x 232 cm) and fits on the extended table. Measure your own table and adjust the runner measurements to suit. The runner can either hang over the end of a table, or lie flat on top of it, whichever you prefer.
- The size of rouleau loops will fit the washers used to make the buttons in this project. If you use larger washers, you will need longer rouleau loops.

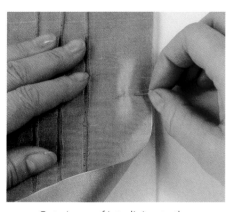

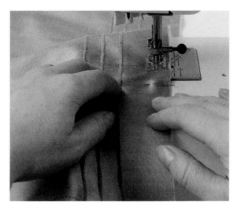

11 Cut pieces of interlining to the same sizes as the runner sections. Lay them flat on the work surface and lay the runner sections right side up on top, aligning the raw edges. Pin the layers together around the edges.

12 Set the sewing machine to the longest straight stitch and baste the layers together right around the edges of each section, stitching within the seam allowance.

13 Cut 18-2⅝ in. (6.5 cm) lengths of rouleau. Fold each in half to make a loop and pin nine to each end of the middle section, aligning the raw ends of the rouleau with the raw edge of the fabric. Measure carefully and check that each loop is opposite the appropriate button on the end sections. Using the sewing machine, baste across the ends of the rouleau, stitching within the seam allowance.

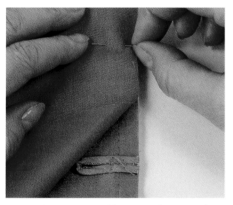

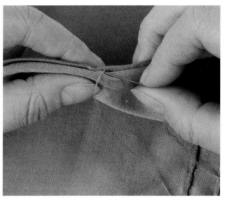

14 Cut a piece of lining to the size of each section of the runner. With right sides facing, lay a piece of lining over the appropriate section and pin the layers together around the edges. Machine stitch the layers together, stitching around the edges of the section taking a ⅝ in. (1.5 cm) seam allowance. Leave a 4 in. (10 cm) opening on one long edge. Repeat for each section.

15 Trim off the corners of each section to reduce the bulk. Turn the sections right side out through the gap left in the stitching. Push all corners through, so that they are square.

16 Slip stitch the gaps closed. Repeat for each section of the runner. Press all the sections. Place each of the rouleau button loops over a corresponding button to assemble the completed runner.

Ideas Gallery fastenings

Buttons and bows are no longer just for little girls. Enjoy these inspirational applications and use your own creative ideas to come up with others!

➤ **Ribbon ties** can be much quicker and easier than fabric ties. Gingham ribbon has been topstitched across the surface of the printed fabric, and becomes integral to the design of the piece. Finish the topstitching close to the edge of the project allowing the ribbon to continue for another 8 in. (20 cm) or so. Be sure that the ribbons on each side are exactly opposite each other. Tie the ends in a bow and trim the ends at an angle.

◀ **Contrasting rouleau loops** can make an interesting feature of button loops. This large gingham check is matched by the smaller check on the buttons to really get the message across.

⋏ **Toggle fastenings** are a great alternative to conventional buttons and buttonholes; consider using cord and simple wooden toggles. The ends of the lengths of cord are threaded through the toggles and the ends of the loops opposite are caught underneath flat cotton tape, which is topstitched in place.

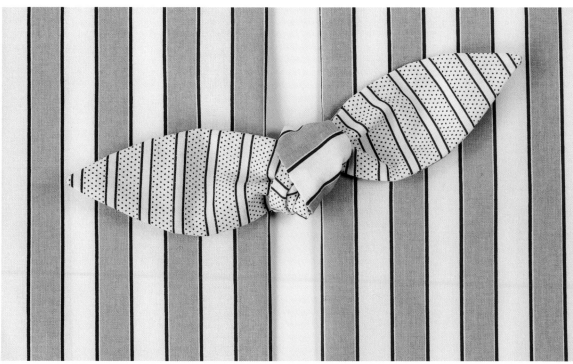

◄ **Shaped fabric ties** are made by cutting out four pieces of fabric in a fish shape. Place each pair right sides together and stitch from the tail along the top of the fish shape and back along the bottom, pivoting at the point. Snip, and turn the shape through. Press the ties. Attach open raw edges to the underside of the project edge; tie.

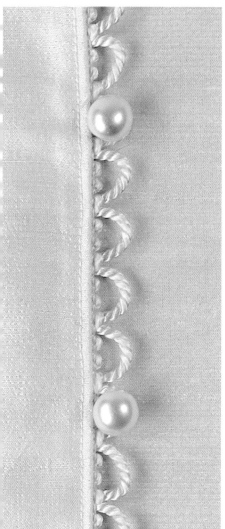

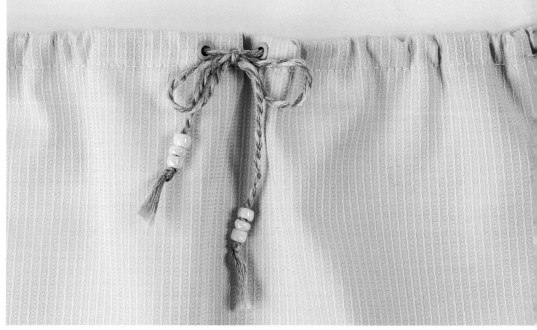

◄ **A purchased loop** trim can be used as an alternative to making fabric loops. In the case of a wedding gown, every loop could be buttoned, but on other projects, it can be nice to leave gaps between the buttons, allowing the loops to form a decorative edge. Place the braid underneath and topstitch close to the edge of the fabric to attach it. Round, pearl-effect buttons will slip very easily through the loops.

⋏ **Casing for a drawstring closures** can be formed at the edge of a garment or other project. Turning the edge twice makes this casing easy and ensures a neat edge. Before topstitching the turning, make holes through which the ends of the cord can pass. Two metal eyelets provide a neat finish, but small buttonholes can also be worked instead.

Templates

Photocopy template(s) to the size specified below. Next trace the template and cut it out carefully. Retain the original copy as a reference.

Flower Pin
Photocopy at 200 percent.

Child's Jumper
Photocopy at 100 percent.

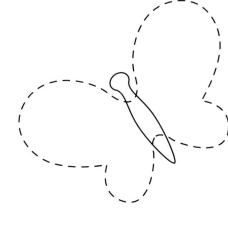

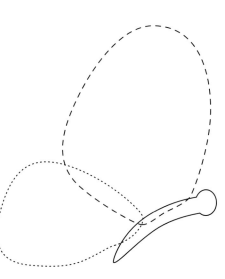

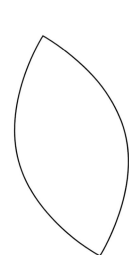

Table Runner, see page 150

These diagrams are to be used as a reference for piecing fabrics together.

Resources

In the United States
Michaels Stores, Inc.
8000 Bent Branch Drive
Irving, TX 75063
Toll-Free Tel: (800) 642-4235
Web: www.michaels.com

Jo-Ann Stores, Inc.
5555 Darrow Road
Hudson, OH 44236
Tel: (330) 656-2600
Web: www.joann.com

In Canada
Fabricland/Fabricville
Over 170 stores from coast to coast in
Canada. For a complete store listing:
Web: www.fabricville.com
(Eastern Canadian shops only)
Web: www.fabricland.com

BB Bargoons
2784 Yonge Street
Toronto, ON M4N 2J2
Tel: 416-481-5273
Web: www.bbbargoons.com

C & M Textiles
7500 St-Hubert
Montreal, QC
H2R 2N6
Tel: 514-272-0247
Web: www.cmtextiles.com

In the United Kingdom
Bead Shop
21a Tower Street
London
WC2H 9NS
Tel: 020 7240 0931
Web: www.beadshop.co.uk

The Button Company
Heritage Buttons Ltd
8 Armadale Road
Chichester, West Suffex
PO19 7NR
Tel: 01243 775462

Cloth House
47 Berwick Street
London
W1F 8SJ
Tel: 020 7437 5155

And also at:
98 Berwick Street
London
W1F 0QJ
Tel: 020 7287 1555
Web: www.clothhouse.com

Creative Beadcraft Ltd.
Unit 2
Asheridge Business Centre
Asheridge Road
Chesham
Buckinghamshire
HP5 2PT
Tel: 01494 778818
Web: www.creativebeadcraft.co.uk

And also at:
20 Beak Street
London
W1F 9RE

Hobbycraft
Tel: 0800 027 2387 for your nearest
branch.
Web: www.hobbycraft.co.uk

John Lewis
Branches nationwide

Kleins
5 Noel Street
London
W1F 8GD
Tel: 020 7437 6162
Web: www.kleins.co.uk

MacCulloch & Wallis
25 - 26 Dering Street
London
W1S 1AT
Tel: 020 7629 0311
Web: www.macculloch-wallis.co.uk

Index

Acknowledgments

Thanks to Katie Cowan and Michelle Lo at Collins & Brown; as always to Kate Haxell, editor extraordinaire; to Matthew Dickens at OnEdition, photographer par excellence, and to Gemma Wilson. Bravo! Many thanks to Luise Roberts for expert advice and assistance with patchwork, and to my mum who burned the midnight oil with me.